Healing the Wounded Spirit

Healing
the
Wounded Spirit

By

LS King

R. C. Linnell Publishing

Healing the Wounded Spirit

ISBN-10:09840025-2-9
ISBN-13: 978-0-9840025-2-8

Published by
R. C. Linnell Publishing
Louisville, Kentucky
www.LinnellPublishing.com

Other publications by LS King:

No Ordinary Woman (ISBN: 978-0-9824373-0-8)
Lady Bray (ISBN: 978-0-9824373-8-4)
Divine Interventions (Coming soon)

Website: *LSKingbooks.com*
Email: *Linda@LSKbooks.com*.

I would like to dedicate this book to:

All my Christian friends who encourage me and pray for my health and success.

Kate Thomas, an author who has been a life long Christian friend and mentor.

My husband Richard, who still loves me despite the many hours I spend on the computer.

Table of Contents

Message From The Author

How many times have we heard that we need to grow thick skin and ignore the things that people may say to our face or behind our back? What does skin have to do with hurting our feelings and making someone feel sad or rejected?

Recently, I ran into an old friend while visiting someone in a hospital. We had had issues in the past, but as adults I felt that we could visit, say hello and make general conversation. In fact, I allowed her the time she needed to visit with our mutual friends and placed myself where we would not be uncomfortable being in the same space. I tried to be an adult as I excused myself and left the room. Within minutes, this person hunted me down and started to belittle me in front of a room full of people. It was obvious that she wanted to hurt me. I asked her to have a seat and she refused. I did everything possible to stop her from saying things about the past. She had no idea what she was talking about because she never got all the facts. She was attacking my family and my siblings were trying to stop her from making a spectacle of both of us. I suggested if she had issues that I would be glad to meet her and discuss them somewhere that was appropriate.

Later I left and went home. I broke down and cried for hours. I was not in any condition to be hit with false, inappropriate remarks that I could not defend. The only thing I could do was walk away and hold in my anger. She had no idea that I had been through a recent emotional breakdown. She had no idea that I had serious health problems. If she had been aware of my recent problems, would she have attacked me like a mad bull? Everyone who witnessed her action was appalled that this was happening. It took days to get over this attack but this experience encouraged me to write this book.

Daily, we walk among people who enjoy making remarks that hurt others mentally, physically and emotionally. It makes us laugh and gives false value to the person who gets a real thrill out of destroying a person in front of others.

 Most of the time, we never see this person as a child of God. We just notice the outside and what people want us to notice. Even little children develop a pecking order as they play with classmates. I have observed children in my kindergarten classroom convince other children that one certain child would not be welcome to the playgroup.

Why is this? Is it because they dress differently? Is it the way they walk or speak? Yes, I definitely know children judge the way others look physically. I have watched physically disfigured children pushed away from playgroups because they look different and are labeled as undesirable. My own child at the age of three noticed that a Korean child looked different from the others in his nursery school class. He walked up to her and looked her in the face as innocent as a three year old could, and asked, "What happened to you?"

We might expect young children to be inquisitive and insulting without knowing that they are hurting feelings, but not adults. Somewhere in life we all learn what is socially acceptable. Even though some things may be unacceptable in God's eyes or in social settings, it is still a part of daily rituals. In the workplace, schools and yes, in churches. There is a pecking order that excludes the handicapped, the poor, the weak and those that are likely to shy away from any kind of confrontation.

What does Jesus see when he looks at the Christian who decides to take the day off and regress into a bully to be socially accepted? Christians do this to participate in the world activities that allow them to belong for maybe a minute, hour or even a day. Do we decide to do this because we know this person has thick skin? "Oh well, he can take it." "Everyone calls him that."

I have noticed that people are increasingly turning to drugs, alcohol, and inappropriate behaviors to mask the feelings that abuse has persuaded them to believe about themselves. Does this make thick skin? Does this enhance the Christian spirit? No! Like the thorns on a rose it only pricks the skin. The pricks in the skin hurt and some stay in the skin for a lifetime. Rejection can turn people toward drugs and alcohol. When you don't feel confident about yourself, it is easy to hide behind the addiction.

It is only in the last few years I have learned that God is the only element in my life that can help me grow the spirit I need to be a better woman, mother, wife, and friend. I always knew that I could go to God but seldom did I take that opportunity to ask Him to grow me as a Christian. Looking back, I should have reached out to God for all the hurts that pricked my skin as a child and as an adult.

How is your Christian spirit? Are you still allowing others to prick your skin and make you bleed? Are you doing the hurting? Be honest, we have each intentionally hurt others. We say things that cause pain, we do things to get revenge, and we secretly bring others into our circle to validate our actions. Life is a gift that should be enjoyed. When we purposely hurt others, then we are not giving the gift of life. People everywhere are silently suffering.

This is why I feel it is important to address the subject of the "wounded spirit." I hope you will benefit from the information or encourage someone who is hurting to read the book. It is my goal to let everyone know that they have worth and power. Our worth does not depend on what others think of us. It is so hard to understand, "If God is for us, who can be against us?"

Psalm 44:4-5

"You are my King and my God. You command victories for your people. Only by Your power can we push back our enemies."

Enjoy reading this book and as you read, "Rejoice and know that you are the child of the King."

This is my fourth book. God has been on this journey with me as I write to inspire others to stand strong against the storms that can destroy any individual.

LS King

Introduction

Do you know who you really are? Look in the mirror and take a peek at the person that you call yourself. You may be blond, brunette, redhead, middle aged, or distinguishably older. You may see yourself as being fat, thin, skinny, plump, or slightly over-or underweight. You may see yourself as tall or short.

You have a name and a gender. Regardless of the sex that you want to be, God has given you a sex. You are either male or female and these are the only two choices. I may not be politically correct, but let's face the facts: God made Adam a man and Eve a woman. He also made them sexually different. It is only in rare cases do we not know at birth if we are male or female. There is no way that God would make a mistake and reverse the roles after birth. So, while looking in the mirror you will notice that you do have a gender, male or female.

At birth, you receive a name. It may be the name given to your mother, father, or grandparents. Whatever your name, it will be totally you and when spoken, you will respond. It took nine months to develop you and use the correct DNA that would bring together all your physical working parts. You belonged to someone. Someone gave birth to you and someone loved you soon after you dropped out of the birth canal. Chances are there were several people waiting for your arrival. You did nothing but cry and coo, and everyone loved you. You had a fan club and when you were home with your parents you were on display for all to hold and love. All you needed was something to eat and someone to keep you warm and dry. It didn't matter to you if you were called names, picked on or put in time out. Crying was your only defense.

As we grow into childhood, we develop aggression to get what we want. It still does not matter if you hurt the child sitting next to you. If you desire his toy, and biting, grabbing or pushing works, you continue to repeat the behavior to satisfy your wants.

Now comes the hard part. When you start school not everyone is going to clap and praise you for your accomplishments. Because we are all different, we will grow at our own rate of development. God knows this but somehow, parents and other children do not understand. You are put on display to be charted and compared to other people that are of the same age and gender. Your physical makeup may be different. Some will be creative and some will be athletic. People begin to notice you for your accomplishments.

Sad, but true, some people are noted as losers because they are not recognized for the popular accomplishment in life. Somehow, we get lost in the world of judgment. We are never told that the only person worthy of judging a person is Christ. Just because we can't see Christ and He doesn't show up at the Friday night ballgames, He doesn't have the best class project, wasn't in the junior or senior play, and never made it to specific parties or groups, some people think that He does not exist. If Jesus Christ is the only judge we need to worry about, then why do we try so hard to please others? I hope this book will open your eyes, help you to heal your wounded spirit and find happiness that we all deserve. Life is too short to worry about the ugly events that happen to each of us. Take one day at a time. Breathe, relax, and learn to love yourself.

Remember: You deserve the best that the world has to offer.

Chapter 1

How Is Your Daily Walk?

When we think about our daily routines, we usually open up images of events that have happened to us throughout the day. This includes places we went, and people we saw or people we talked with. Routines are especially strong when we work a nine-to-five job that brings us into the same setting day after day. How much do we influence these individuals with the way we talk, think or listen? How often do we stop and pray for the people we see on a daily basis? This includes the obnoxious co-worker who is constantly getting on everyone's nerves. When we are inconvenienced, we become selfish. How often do you pass an EMS truck going down the street and become disgusted because you have to pull over to the side of the road and wait a few minutes before you can continue to your destination? What about the neighbor next door, who is always catching you just as you drive into the driveway after work and wants to talk ball scores or tell you insignificant things that happened in the neighborhood during the day? What about the people on your answering machine that you had promised you would call back and you intentionally avoid them because they demand your time and attention?

Any person may be an inconvenience for you, but they are individuals who at some point in life have a story. The co-worker might be lonely, feeling lost or incomplete. The person in the EMS ambulance obviously needs medical attention in a hurry. The neighbor may need the assurance that someone cares enough to listen to what he thinks is important information. The telephone messages may be something you dread. However, if you promise someone that you will do something and fail to follow through with your commitment, it will show your true personality.

Losing your temper and yelling at someone because they are who they are, is not in your favor. God wants us to walk daily the same way we walk when we are in church giving a testimony to other Christians about something that God led us to do or say. A daily Christian walk is very important and it is one of the hardest things that we have to do each day. One little comment can take you from hero to zero and you can damage a person's self-esteem for life.

So many times, I have put people up on a pedestal. I look at a person and feel that they have all the right answers. This is so wrong. Pray before you make decisions. Taking an opinion from others can be very dangerous. Maybe a friend tells you that she wouldn't go on a trip or visit a certain friend. Don't let friends change your mind. We can find a thousand reasons to allow others to influence our daily walk. Always do what you feel is important to you.

Look at the example of Ruby and Donna:

"Just don't speak to her," said Ruby as she passed the front desk where Donna was getting on everyone's nerves explaining how she got twenty percent off her purchase at Wal-Mart.

"If you don't say 'good morning' to her she will not start one of her stories. That's the way I have handled it for years," said Ruby. "I just walk right by her and she knows that I am not going to give her the time of day."

Is this what Jesus would have done? Is this your daily walk? What about telling the truth? What if Ruby had said the following:

"Hi, Donna, hope you have a lovely day. I would love to stop and chat, but frankly I am in a rush and maybe we can talk some other time."

Why can't we just be honest and tell the truth? Are you aware of the feelings that you plant inside the heart and soul of others? Are you taking the time to show kindness? Do you smile and bring a pleasant atmosphere to those around you?

We look at people and their physical features and immediately we put what we see into our little computers and draw a conclusion about that person. This allows us to make a judgment about their lifestyle. We tend to ask ourselves, "Can this person carry on a conversation? What opinion will others make when they see me with this person?" If you decide not to be friends with this person based on looks, you just might be missing out on a lifelong friend.

Judging others on a physical basis is done every day: walking down the street, watching people in a mall, looking across a room, watching others eat at a restaurant. We all do this without thinking. It is our nature to want to talk to approachable people, yet remain distant from those who are different.

Working with young children is certainly a challenge. They will ask the real questions. Once, a child asked me why I had a big mole on my face. Taking it to heart, I asked my dermatologist about it when he was removing a spot on my arm. He replied, "Yes, you are too pretty to have that huge mole on your face and I am going to do something about it today." I then became conscious of my physical appearance and the acne that may or may not be a part of my normal facial features.

Another one of my students described me as having blue eyebrows. Knowing he did not know the word for shadow, I realized that I was wearing too much eye shadow. If you want the truth just ask a child.

I remember as a child I had to wear corrective shoes. I do not have an arch and never will. It was the opinion of my mother that I should see a foot doctor at an early age. He suggested I wear corrective shoes with built-in arches. There were only two types of shoes made with arches. They were either brown and white or black and white. They had a Thomas heel that pushed my knees into place so my feet would fall back into the shoe when laced tightly. Each day I wore those shoes to school with white socks and a dress. We were not allowed to wear pants to school until I was a senior in high school. One day, a mean-spirited boy in my class made fun of me.

"Girl, why do you always wear those big old ugly shoes to school?"

I was so embarrassed that I did not answer. From that day on I would walk into my classroom from the front door and never go out the back door where his desk was located. I cried each day to my mother asking her to please let me wear normal shoes. She was convinced that the only way I was ever going to have perfect feet was to be bound tightly into that type of shoe. When I became a freshman in high school I did win the battle and had supports made for my popular Weejuns. That has been way over forty years ago and I still remember that nasty comment.

I remember the school volunteers calling out our names and weight when they did the health exams in school. It was humiliating to be one of the largest girls in the class. I lived with the word "fat" and still do. Later in life, the girl who haunted me the most saw me at the state fair when I was working for one of the TV stations handing out ads on free bags. When she approached me at the desk, she looked at my friends and made one last remark:

"Wow, I went to high school with her and you should have seen how fat she was."

It still rings in my ears. I suppose it was a compliment since I had lost over thirty pounds after high school, but I still saw it as a remark that should not have been repeated. Negative remarks always hurt no matter how old you are.

Your daily walk says a lot about who you are and what you believe. It also says a lot about your values. Is Christ the person in your life that you want to impress? Are you living a Christian example in your daily walk? Where are you going and where have you been? Think about it daily. Who are you when you look into a mirror? Check out the feelings you have for yourself and your loved ones. Don't allow anyone to hurt one of God's children. Walk daily with God by your side and He will show you the way to grow positive healthy attitudes. It's all about your spirit. Try to develop a spirit that glows and gives a warm smile to individuals you meet. Surprisingly, people will smile back and you will be blessed. Remember, if you know where you are going, you can enjoy the journey.

With a positive attitude and a sweet spirit, the only place we can go is up. Make the best of each day.

God bless you and may your daily journeys be happy ones.

Ephesians 4: 17-18 (NIV)

"So I tell you this, and insist on it in the Lord, that you must no longer live as the Gentiles do, in the futility of their thinking."

"They are darkened in their understanding and separated from the life of God because of the ignorance that is in them due to the hardening of their hearts."

Learn to love one another as Christ loves us.

Chapter 2

Take Control of Your Mind

Daily, we are brainwashed with what we see on TV and hear on the radio. Most of this propaganda is designed to tell you lies about who you are and who you think you want to be. If you buy a certain product, you will look like a certain movie star. If you cook a certain food or drink a certain drink, you are in the "in" crowd. It's all about playing with the mind of those who may be watching or listening to the media. People get paid to lie to us. If you buy into those types of ideas, you will certainly come to believe that you will never measure up to what society thinks is normal.

There are hours of training and taping and producing commercials that lie to God's people. Just think: What if we spent all that time and energy telling people that God is the only hope for a happy, healthy, cleansing, guilt free lifestyle? I can just see it now.

Guilt Free Lifestyle

You can't get it in a bottle or buy it at the store, but you can find it right in front of you in your daily devotions, led by the Holy Spirit. It is free to anyone who will acknowledge that Jesus Christ died on the cross for our sins and He is ready to make you one of His followers today. The price of this product is free.

Yes, ladies and gentlemen, when was the last time you were given a free item with no strings attached?

So, you don't believe me? You think it's a gimmick?

Well, watch this, Just as this stain remover takes away the stains from your favorite shirt, Christ has died on the cross to take away all your stains and He promises that if you use the verses in His Word, the Bible, you, too can be stain free and have everlasting life.

Yes, **Guilt-Free Lifestyle**! This product will improve your sleep, give your spirit a lift, help you meet new friends and bring you back to life.

You can throw away your anxiety medication, and save the money you spend on all those products that make you more desirable to those around you.

The new friends you make will not judge you. They will love you just the way you are.

With this product you will get your very own Bible that will give you more promises that I don't have time to tell you about.

The Bible will explain everything you need to know about how and why you look the way you do. It will also explain the plan for your life: Where you are going and how you will get there.

Now I know this sounds silly, but this is just what we see on a daily basis as we drive down the street and see billboards advertising the best places to be entertained. We listen to the radio, TV and now the Internet to find out what products we should be using. Most of these advertisements are lies. I must admit that they do have cute little jingles and I find myself singing them long after the commercial has ended. This is what the advertiser wants us to do. An interesting person gets on the screen and gives testimonies that make the TV audience pick up the phone and dial right away hoping to get one chance to buy the product before the price goes up. "And if you call right now we will throw in this special gift."

It is amazing how fast we can dial for a special gift that might be only a sponge or a key chain.

But, back to our product: **Guilt-Free Lifestyle.** I truly think that we could market this product to those who are looking for a way out of the guilt and shame they have allowed themselves to carry around for years. Look at it the way a television producer would:

> ➢ **We could have testimonials about our product:**

Recipients of our product could go on TV and radio to promote **Guilt-Free Lifestyle** and tell how it changed their outlook on every aspect of their life. It might go like this:

"I tried **Guilt-Free Lifestyle** and today I can honestly say that I feel free from the chains of life. I no longer pick fights with friends and spend money to drink my worries away. I look younger and have decided to follow the written word in the Bible. Everything it says is true! I have more love for my hateful friends. I just say that I am sorry you're mad at life, but remember God still loves you."

➤ **We could show before and after:**

"Before **Guilt-Free Lifestyle,** I was angry at the world, thought God had forsaken me, needed revenge, and hated to see what the next day would bring in my life. Now, I can even wake with a prayer on my lips, sing a pleasant song and share the gospel with friends that I don't even enjoy being with."

➤ **We could try the bandwagon method of jumping on board today.**

"I feel like my heavy load has been lifted as I pray for everything and everyone who I see with needs. I am having fun in life." What about you? Do you think you would like to get rid of your heavy load? Just pick up the Bible and read about Jesus and you, too, can have **Guilt-Free Lifestyle.**"

Would you buy this product? I write this tongue-in-cheek. It does help to believe, but people need to take an honest look at themselves.

I confess that my biggest problem in life has been guilt. Why do we punish ourselves by feeling guilty, wondering if we hurt someone's feelings by something we said or did? We evaluate our statements worrying if we said enough or if we said the right thing. For example, we might question the following in our minds:

❖ "Did I hurt Sandy's feelings? She didn't speak to me in club today."

❖ "I can't make the baby shower and I feel so guilty that I must somehow make it up to Peggy and her mom. Maybe I'll call her and apologize or take her out for lunch."

So much in life are feelings we bring on ourselves because we let others make us feel guilty. When they know you will take on the guilt, they will lay on the guilt. Do not put yourself out there with feelings that may or may not involve you.

Many times, we do this with our spouses. We know just where and when to place the guilt. Does this sound familiar?

Wife: "Oh, so you would rather go to the car show

than be with me?"

Husband: "No supper again tonight? What have you

done all day?"

I am sure each of us has played the trump card when it comes to getting what we want. I really think if we sell a product like **Guilt-Free Lifestyle,** it should come with a disclaimer.

Caution! When you buy this product, the devil will try to enter your mind and continue to speak to you repeatedly until you become a captive soul that he can control. Be sure you read the written Word daily to keep him at bay.

This caution reminds us that we are human and will fail from time to time. Just do not give up. Here are a few verses that will help you keep these self-punishing thoughts out of your heart and mind:

2 Corinthians: 10-5 (NIV)

"We must learn to bring every thought into captivity."

Philippians 2:5 (NIV)

"Your attitude should be the same as that of Christ Jesus."

Mark 7:21-22 (NIV)

"For from within, out of men's heart, come evil thoughts, sexual immorality, theft, murder, adultery, greed, malice, deceit, lewdness, envy, slander, arrogance and folly."

We are all sinners, born with a fallen nature, so don't be too hard on yourself when you fail to live up to God's standards. Don't be afraid to admit to God that you have failed. Repent and ask forgiveness using your experience to be wary of other times that you might make the same mistake. God wants us to learn from our sins and our mistakes. He knows we are human and we are not free of sin. Praise God for His Grace that will allow us to ask for forgiveness.

Romans 3:23

"For all have sinned and fallen short of the Glory of God."

We need daily victory over the world. If we understand salvation, we will understand that when we accept Christ into our life it is the beginning and not the end.

Romans: 5:8 (NIV)

"And God demonstrated his love for us and yet while we were sinners Christ died for us."

Knowing that Christ died for us, we should not put anything in the place of God. He should be all we need to satisfy our needs. We have to learn to stand apart from those who try to separate us from Christ. Remember that sin always costs something and so we must never doubt God. We should always stand on His Word. Worship should be a daily activity where you seek God. Worship should be an attitude of the heart. Worship should have an impact on every part of our lives. God is always available and nothing is impossible with God.

Chapter 3

If God Turned Us Inside Out,

What Would We See?

I think it is important to learn who you really are on the inside. If we never let down our guard and let others see our struggle with elements in life, then we will never get support. We will never know love that is designed to help and protect us from others that are hurting us. Sometimes the secrets you hold in your life are killing you. You may have an addiction. You may struggle with mental, sexual or physical abuse. You may have a past that haunts you and makes it hard to be around certain people. God tells us that it is possible to change and make your future brighter. Seeking professional help is not a bad thing. The person you choose should have proper credentials and reflect your values.

Across a crowded room we see many faces and we have no idea what is inside the very inner soul of people who are only faces to our visual eye. We cannot tell if a person comes to every ballgame to get away from a homelife that is demeaning and full of parental or spousal abuse. We can't see the hurt of a little girl who asks Santa to bring her father back home to live in their family. We don't know if single women and men who are looking for honest relationships, are honest and caring. In fact, we know nothing about people we just visually see.

Seldom do we take the time to make friends or pickup on conversations shared with us in hopes that we will be the person who can help with secrets of the heart. Instead, we brag about our life, how much we spend and what we obtain in life. We are quick to ask questions like, "Where is your husband tonight?" This can be hurtful, especially when the person sitting with you at all the school events has never been present with a spouse. It is all in how you make your statement and present it to the person who is listening to your stories.

God wants us to care about others, but we must be careful not to judge or hurt someone's feelings and give advice that will damage the person who is already hiding a secret inside.

Now, what if we could see the person from the inside out?

We would see all the scars from broken hearts, the welts from abuse, and the shame from hiding forbidden secrets. We could see the bruises that bullies made in your life and the cuts of insecurities that make a person miserable in childhood and adulthood.

Would we treat a person the same way if we could see the effects that life had left on them? If we knew the past hurts?

Unfortunately, self-esteem is not tattooed on our arms so others can see if it is high, med, low or very low. We do not have "Fragile, Handle with Care" written on our foreheads. What would we do if we could see that sign on someone we, ourselves, had treated unjustly? Could we say, "I am sorry?" Would this make it better? Unfortunately, we can never take back the harsh statements that hurt others.

The brain is a very complicated organ. It records information and saves it to the hard drive that we call our soul. This hard drive saves our unique collection of opinions that others have handed down to us over the years. Wouldn't it be wonderful if we could go back and erase all the bad memories that project negative thoughts and images we have about ourselves?

If we could just take the broken spirit back to God, He could give us the grace to live with a new image that would bring hope and understanding.

God gives us that promise. We just fail to believe in His Word. We fail to believe Him when He says He cares about everything that happens to His people.

James 1:12-13

"God blesses the people who patiently endure testing. Afterward they will receive the crown of life that God has promised to those who love Him. And remember no one who wants to do wrong should ever say God is tempting me. God never tempted people to do wrong."

Hebrews 13:5

"For God says, 'I will never fail you,' and 'I will never forsake you.'"

Reading this encourages the broken spirit and reminds us that God is always there in times of disgrace, embarrassment, and hurt. He hears and sees the wrong that people pass on to others. He knows what you are feeling and He can help you dissolve the hurt that is making your life miserable. Think positive and you can have a new beginning.

What does it take to start a New Beginning? What does it take to see your life as you interact with cruel hateful people? Remember to stand up for what you believe. Keep the following in mind.

➢ Look toward God and become strong in His Word. I say this because, without a doubt, we can trust that He loves us.

➢ Know that you are a child of God and He made you for a purpose.

➢ God will provide you with the resources to believe in yourself.

➢ Remember: There will come a day of judgment when all will be judged according to God's Word. God will have His time with those who are not Christians and prey on the weak and innocent.

➢ Remember you are never alone.

We will all face the enemy sometime in our life. We all hurt from the things people say and the way we are treated. Parents, be careful, when you correct your children. Harsh words can be a lifelong punishment.

Not knowing how much the words would sting my ears and hurt my feelings, my mother would say:

"I know you are not real smart, but you can at least make good grades in conduct."

I proved her wrong when I finished graduate school, constantly on the Dean's list.

Encourage your children and let them know that you believe in them. They will learn to believe in themselves. Goodnight kisses and hugs for no reason are very important. Time is precious and when you validate your child by spending time with him or her, it will be something that will be remembered for a lifetime.

Make dates with your kids while they are young. Soon they will turn into teenagers who are embarrassed to be seen with you. Treasure each moment and make them learning experiences. Show love to your children and they will show you the same respect and love.

Someday you may need them to listen to you. Age tends to creep upon us and we repeat the same uninteresting story many times. Remember, they will be picking out your nursing home.

Chapter 4

How and Why Do People Develop Negative Opinions?

I am going to explain the building of biased opinions from a teacher's point of view. It was easy for me to accept my class list because I was a kindergarten teacher and I did not have the other teachers telling me what each student could and could not do. I was the first person to take all the children in my classroom blindly. I say blindly, because I had no idea where they came from or what they were able to accomplish.

If you receive a group of children who had already passed the first or second grade, it was always the rule of thumb that you conference with the teacher from the year before and find out who your discipline problems would be, who had good learning skills, and who would probably be in your low reading group. This could be a biased opinion, from only one person, but some students were handed down from grade to grade with a reputation that would stick to them without being given a chance to prove themselves.

Unlike the other teachers, on the first day of school I accepted each child on equal terms. I only knew their names and their birthdays. I had no school records to compare. They were all little people with wide eyes and enthusiasm. One by one, I gave them a chance to share what they could about their home or family, encouraging them to tell about their summer vacation. Information put a name and story with a face. Some stories I remembered and some I forgot. At the end of the day, I gathered up their information sheets to review at home.

As weeks passed each child unfolded like a butterfly opening its wings. There were children on free lunches and some living with grandparents. There were children with poor attendance and children with no father at home. There were children with excellent behavior and some who clearly did not know the skills necessary for their age and stage of development.

One can plainly see that some children have an advantage over others because they have been given opportunities to experience life at home playing learning games and preparing for the first year in school. Some children will know how to talk their way into situations that will allow them to be friends with more privileged friends. Parents who try to make school fun by purchasing new erasers that look like dolls or cars and markers and pencils that glow in the dark are not giving their child an advantage. At this age, most children are clueless about making friends. They will share all of their special school supplies to make friends. Soon they will learn the true definition of friendship the hard way.

The word "share" will take on a new meaning for each child. It was common to have parents call and ask what happened to Johnny's new item brought especially for school and placed in his brand-new backpack.

Life lessons begin in kindergarten. It was my job to teach what is and what is not appropriate to do in the classroom. The children have to learn that sharing is not taking or possessing. I had to handle each child with care. I taught all children at the same speed, knowing there would be some individuals who would need extra help to develop mentally, socially and physically. Now, instead of an equal group of young children, I had several groups who had different needs. I spent ten months with them and I knew them without turning around to see who is standing at my desk asking for help. I learned their innermost thoughts and problems.

Individually they trusted me with stories from home and asked me questions because they learned that I cared. Each child shared surprising events with me and I tried not to judge them. I questioned them and gave them advice. I may have been the only person in their short lives that they could trust. My daily walk was measured and recorded. This was my job as a kindergarten teacher. It was what I signed up to do.

When they advanced to another grade they were wiser and had learned to cover up their feelings. They did not trust anyone for they had learned that life was not fair.

As Christians, we should be open to others as if they were the innocent kindergarten student away at school for the first time. Give people the chance to tell their story. Be kind to those who walk a different way and allow the Christian spirit to show others that we can be trusted. Remember: Someday we will be accountable for the way we treat others.

Chapter 5

Suck It Up and Forget It

How many times have your kids come to you and complained that someone hurt their feelings? In response did you look at them and say, "Oh, just suck it up and forget it. Don't be a baby." Did you ever realize that when you make this statement, you are telling your child that he is not worthy of your time to fix the problem? This is a negative statement that could last for a lifetime.

Jesus doesn't say, "Suck it up and go on." Jesus tells our children that they should show respect to others. They must learn right from wrong and how to choose the correct option. As parents, there are some things we can do to help them:

- ✓ Teach them that if they do wrong there will be consequences. It is important to admit that they have done wrong and learn what is expected.

- ✓ Communicate with your children. Get to know their friends. Get to know how they feel about events that are taking place in their lives.

- ✓ Spend time with your children and make a time for the family to have fun together.

- ✓ Provide direction.

- ✓ Let your children develop their own personal identity. Show them their strengths.

- ✓ Praise them often for making right decisions.

- ✓ Teach your children how to attack problems in a positive way.

- ✓ Tell your children that it is normal to remember the person or event that hurt them. It is okay to be angry, but God says that we must forgive the person.

Psalm 25: 1-2

"To you, O Lord, I lift up my soul. I trust in you my God! Do not let my enemies rejoice in my defeat?"

When we remind others that God gives us worth, we can truly have the assurance that other's negative opinions are not worthy of our ears.

Psalm 25: 3

"No one who trusts in you will ever be disgraced, but disgrace comes to those who try to deceive others."

There are so many people who do suck it up and continue to allow certain situations to make them miserable. Words and rejection can cut deeply causing the body to bleed the joy out of your life. We often get so used to the attack that we expect the abuse whenever we are around the situation. Soon we have no joy left in life. Without joy, there is no way to become a faithful loving, caring Christian. We need the strength and the joy of the Lord to be a Christian willing to share the Word and work in the body of Christ called the church. Without joy, we lose hope and faith.

God wants all of us to stay away from those who abuse us and drain us until we lose hope of ever living a joyful, happy life. We must always remember to reject the people and lifestyle that hurts us and takes away a chance to inherit the happiness that only God can provide.

Psalm 69:4

"Those who hate me without cause are more numerous than the hairs on my head. These enemies who seek to destroy me are doing so without cause. They attack me with lies, demanding that I give back what I didn't steal."

We learn that God tells us that there are those who will hate us without cause. Some will try to destroy us without cause. There are people who are controllers, pleasers, victims, and charmers.

Most women are pleasers. History shows us that women have been corrected and directed by men for centuries. This has caused low self-esteem. Women feel like servants who have no right to think on their own. They feel that they are not doing their best because they are never given the praise they deserve when they are productive.

Women feel that they are responsible for the happiness of others. This then makes them victims. The victim does not see value from within. They have to perform to be accepted by others. They feel that God is always judging them and not others.

Charmers know how to make others feel good about bad decisions. They tell people what they want to hear and use lies to tempt good people to join in bad activities. Remember that the devil is a wonderful charmer.

When you feel that the world has let you down and people hurt you, it is okay to cry or show emotion. Not only should we cry, but we should also cry out to Christ. Know that God is there and He wants you to tell Him your feelings.

- Remember to hate what is evil.

- Cling to what is good.

- Devote yourself to others with brotherly love.

- Honor one another with what is good about us.

Finding another Christian to share in your love of Christ is one of the most wonderful gifts from God. Together you can lift up Christ and share daily devotions that will encourage self-esteem. Put on the Lord Jesus Christ. Shut down the demands of the world and take every opportunity to love as Jesus did.

Romans 14:10

"So why do you condemn another Christian? Remember, each of us will stand personally before the judgment seat of God ."

Romans 14:13

"So don't condemn each other anymore. Decide instead to live in such a way that you will not put an obstacle in another Christian's path."

God does not give up on His people and certainly does not suggest that we "suck it up and go on." When we allow others to control our lives to the point where we are not able to enjoy life, it will chip away at the person God made. Control will also erode away at the person that God wants to do His work. God chose to love and bless every person with his Holy Spirit. If you learn to "suck it up and go on," you become bitter and there is no way others can see God in you.

When we ignore the problem and just "suck it up and go on," we learn to reject our feelings. We do not know how to be true to ourselves. We are abandoning important parts of ourselves and we take on the thoughts and feelings of others around us.

Instead, God says that we must be self-controlled and alert. Know the enemy and confront him or her about the evil they are displaying. Never live in fear of people, places, or things. Fear is a one-way message that will convince you that you have no power over difficult situations. Remember, you have the power to say, "I will not go there, I will not build you up to others with lies, and I will not give things to be accepted." If you do not feel comfortable with a situation, stand up for what you believe. Letting others control you is a form of abuse.

Remember that we must trust the Lord and claim Him as our Savior. Sometimes this is the only way we can properly heal from abuse. Understanding that someone loves us unconditionally, affirms that you do possess the power to make your own decisions. Even if we make the wrong decision, God will still love us. The difference is in knowing that you can always pray about your decision and read what God wants from you. His word is always available for reference.

Chapter 6

Becky's Story

I have a close friend who grew up with me in church. We enjoyed our youth by going on trips, attending youth events and hanging out at ballgames on the weekends. Several weekends she would end up spending the night at my house with a group of girlfriends laughing, doing hair, polishing our nails and swimming late at night in our pool. At the age of twenty, we were all still single and living at home. Becky (not her real name) was a few years older than the rest of the group. She had finished school and was working at a hospital making her own money. She was the first to drive, so we would pile into her car and run around town looking for men who were single, fun and good-looking.

The local men's softball games proved to be a great place to meet single guys. We all had our favorite male friends and we would cheer them on as they went to bat. After the games, we would go to a small hangout and sit outside and enjoy listening to music. It was surely an innocent time for girls who were just looking for fun. Becky fell in love with one of the men who gave her attention and soon learned that he was only interested in her as a friend, not a long-term relationship.

This broke her heart, but she learned that true love does not come for only a season. Unfortunately, she never learned what true love looks and feels like.

Becky came from an abusive situation. Her father was an army sergeant and controlled his home by playing the sergeant role. Her mother jumped to every order given by her husband. He set rules and regulations that were ridiculous. I remember that Becky got in trouble for having her dresser drawer open three inches because she left in a hurry to go to work. He walked through the house and checked out the rooms of each adult child who was still living at home. He also charged rent. Children were not allowed to use the air conditioner and he controlled the heat. He cooked all the food and he had a list for the groceries that had to be ready for him when he arrived home. Becky's mother also lived in fear of her husband. He was never abusive to her physically that I know about, however, the whole family waltzed around the head of the house, "Daddy."

Becky had a curfew of eleven o'clock. She also had a time limit on the phone when her father was home. It was a stressful time for her when she was trying to build a life for herself. She quickly learned to keep secrets from her father and followed her mother's instructions. When Becky arrived home from work each day, she soon learned whether her father was in a good mood. Her mother would caution her to be quiet and tread lightly because her father was mad about something. He wanted to be in control of everything in his home.

Becky met a man at work and soon he was giving her attention she desperately craved. Within a year, she was dating. We all met this young man and learned he was someone who would lie to get attention.

He wanted to be the center of attention. He was a controlling man just like her father. We tried to tell her that he seemed like a good person, but not the type of husband that she would be happy living with the rest of her life. Becky would not listen. She continued to date him and we were all in her wedding.

Becky's husband was older and soon he was taking control of her entire life. He would yell at her if she didn't cook, or come home directly from work. She worked all the overtime she could to support the family. His job was not paying what they needed financially. He refused to take on a second job. Every night at bedtime, she had to stop what she was doing and fix him a bologna sandwich, with a cupcake and a Pepsi. If these items were not in stock, she would have to drive to the grocery to obtain them.

The money problem only got worse. He would buy new cars and items that were not in their budget. Becky ended up paying monthly payments on items that they could not afford. This made Becky work harder and put in more hours in the hospital. They had two children and Becky would put them to bed and go back to work to get overtime. There was little time spent with her children. They were very smart and so homework came easy. However, Becky was not aware who their friends were or where they were hanging out. Her husband, on the other hand, would also leave home to be with his friends at various places.

She had lost all control of her family. She attended church whenever she was not working and always took her children. Becky's husband never attended church with his family. He did not like going to church and so this gave him more time to do what he wanted when she was away at church dinners or a church service.

As years passed, Becky could not be her own person. She would always be upset about something her husband had said or done around her parents and friends. Becky was always in a hurry. She lost touch with all her friends. She did not know who she was and what God had planned for her. She kept a full schedule and it never included her friends.

Becky took care of her parents when they could no longer drive and take care of their own needs. On her days off from work, she would take her mother to the hairdresser and her father to the doctor. They always had a list of items and duties for her to complete.

Her older daughter left home at the age of eighteen. Becky was not even aware that she was living with a friend. Busy with work and trying to satisfy the needs of her husband and parents, Becky totally lost touch with her children. The girls were good students and were always home so Becky thought that her daughter was studying at a friend's house at night. When the realization hit Becky, she was devastated. She questioned why this happened, and found out that her child felt that she was abused and never given the opportunity to be a part of a real family. Slowly, she was moving her clothes out of the house and into a friend's house. Pretending that she was invited for sleepovers and tutoring sessions, the older daughter was gone and there was nothing Becky could do about it.

It has been over fifteen years and Becky has not seen or heard from her elder child. Becky grieves and hopes daily to see or hear something positive from the daughter she gave birth to and loved so much. How could all of this have happened right in front of her eyes? The younger child will never be able to share life with the older sibling. Becky's older daughter is now in the same abusive lifestyle. She left school and moved in with a controlling man who monitors her every movement. She is held captive in his house. Becky's daughter told a friend that she is only allowed to go to work and go to the doctor when he gives her permission.

It is a sad story. Just like her mother, Becky's daughter was looking for someone to take care of her. The daughter's boyfriend has warned Becky and her husband to stay away from their daughter. Afraid to go to the police, they have not attempted to contact her. She has chosen to live with a man that her mother and father have never known. We are shocked that Becky has listened to her husband and has not addressed the situation. Becky's daughter threatens to report her parents as abusers if they go to the police or try to contact her.

As the years passed, life has never changed for Becky. It has only gotten harder. Her husband was dismissed from his job and Becky is responsible for paying the bills and putting her youngest child through school. Her husband still gives her a guilt trip if she does anything that he does not like. She never has the house clean enough to please him and there is never enough food for him to eat in the house.

He seldom shops for the house and leaves when she could use a helping hand. Bills are still there to be paid, a little at a time, when she can afford to spare a few dollars to keep the bill collectors away. Her husband is able to work but says that there are no jobs where he can make the money he needs to help the family. He also claims that people are not hiring men his age. He makes any excuse to keep from working.

I tell you this story because this is a prime example of what we, as women, have learned from our mothers. Just like Becky, her mother wanted to make sure her husband was never irritated or upset. She felt responsible for his happiness. She made sure each child followed the house rules and everything would go as planned. The damage Becky's mother and father have done to their daughter will never be acknowledged. She always wanted Becky to, "Suck it up and forget it." This was her definition of a good mother and a wonderful wife.

Becky is still living this life. Her health is bad and she will never be able to retire when her age will allow her. She hates her husband and has bitterness for her mother, who she feels responsible for since her father's death. Weekly, Becky spends her time ministering to her mother's needs and ignoring her own. There has never been any consideration for Becky's needs.

Becky is empty. She has nothing left to give. She has no time for pleasure. The joy was bled out of her life. Becky does not see a way out and will never learn that God does not intend for her to be unhappy. She has never learned that she is not responsible for her husband's happiness. Buying things will not make him happy and has only put a strain on the family budget. She does not allow time for herself. Her clothes and hair are unkempt, making her an easy target for gossip from the women at work.

Not knowing what Becky has been through, they will talk about her and tease her and she will not fight back. She is a wonderful person and she would never hurt anyone's feelings. When no one wants to follow up on a job that is difficult or time-consuming, they will give the job to Becky, knowing that she will do the job and not complain. Advancement and pay raises have gone to coworkers who only have a few years of experience. Becky's boss knows that she will not complain or report it to the company. She has cried to me as she watches others with less experience get the good jobs. Becky is honest. She has not learned how to beat the system and flatter the boss to get job promotions.

As her good friend, I get sick just writing this story. I love this friend and there are no words or books that I can give her to change her idea of what a good Christian woman looks like. She has been conditioned to believe that what she is doing is what God wants for her. She will say to me, "Someday when we get to Heaven, we will be happy." She has destroyed her life and there is no joy living within her.

I listen as she cries out to me and thanks me for being a good friend. I give advice and pray with her, but years of abuse can not be erased easily. I have given her books about codependency and she understands the problem but is afraid to change her life.

I wonder how many people are living the same lie? They suffer in silence thinking they are doing what God wants from them.

Becky did not choose a godly husband. Together they did not build their family around Christ and what He expects from us as Christian parents. It is important when couples decide to have children, not only to choose the best place to raise them, but to choose the best way to raise them.

The family was the first institution built by God. A couple starting a family needs to think about the godly heritage that they need to build in their house. Both parents must make this decision and they should support and honor each other equally. Some things to consider are:

> Is the house protected from the corrupt language and sin located right outside its doors?

> Is the house full of prayer and positive experiences?

> Do we allow God's Word to flow throughout the house as we teach right from wrong?

> Is there contentment in the house? Is it a place that the family longs to gather for love and security?

When we build a godly home, we will be blessed. This is what God wants from each of us. He wants us to be happy in our marriages and in our homes. When we become codependent on someone or something, we are not pleasing God.

Chapter 7

The Journey

We are all on a journey. Some of us carry more bundles than others. Some of us carry heavier bundles. Carrying these bundles makes us slow in our stride. It stops us from making the necessary steps it takes to get to our final destination. Sometimes we are encouraged to put down the load or leave it behind so the walk will be easier. Taking the load away will allow the body and soul to relax. Rest from the burden will make the time spent on the journey fresh and new.

Hearing the suggestion is not reason enough for most people to leave the heavy bundles behind. They have carried the load too long. When it is placed safely behind, there are those who still feel the need to go back and pick it up again. Even when we learn that we need to move out of a destructive pattern into a healthier situation, we make a halfhearted attempt to lose the load.

It is only when we decide deep within us that we want to change are we truly able to make the necessary move to put down the heavy load and run freely and enjoy life's journey.

When you fail to lighten the load there is no way you can give from your inner soul and be the person God wants you to be. Everyone needs to find spiritual freedom. We need the freedom to connect with God and read His Word. It is a freedom to enjoy the creation that God has given us through nature. We need the freedom to listen to what God has to say to us when we ask for answers through prayer. We need the freedom to sing and rejoice in the Lord, while connecting with the Holy Spirit. Spiritual freedom will allow you to shed pride and insecure attitudes that mask relationships with God.

It is important that we learn to lighten the load and find serenity. In today's world, we are always on guard, afraid that others will recognize that we might be doing something unacceptable. People are worried that they might not be good enough, giving enough, or prepared enough. We struggle to survive the events of the daily routines stuffed into twenty-four hours. We try to keep up with the neighbors and friends by enrolling our children in afterschool programs, weekend sports, play dates and birthday parties. We spend priceless time making cupcakes for organizations that do not matter and volunteering to be on committees that plan parties that will not be remembered in five years. When do we find serenity?

When we spill out our energy to everyone around us, we end up being empty. Just like my friend Becky. She is always giving and she never allows herself time to fill her cup. We are not productive when we are emotionally, spiritually and physically empty. Learn to take time to rest so you can make the best of life.

If women could justify the time off, I am sure they would try to find the time to be alone. Unfortunately, they feel that it is a waste of money and time, and being alone is selfish and unproductive. Wait! What is wrong with solitude? Why can't we look inward for strength?

I remember feeling alone and disillusioned when I became an empty nester. I woke in the morning and found that my job as a mother was gone. I was alone until my husband came home from work. I fixed a big dinner and then realized it was unnecessary for just two of us. My husband loved it but I missed the noise of friends coming and going through our back door. I walked through the house and looked for signs of life in my son's room. I took notice of the baby pictures that had been hanging on the wall for twenty years. "What has happened here?" I questioned.

Day after day I cried inside because I felt the empty emotions that I, as a woman, had hidden behind activities concerning my children. Suddenly, my past began to surface and I was hyperventilating, thinking about what I missed as a child growing up. Sad memories of my childhood made me cry. I began to realize that I had no family. My parents were dead, my mother-in-law and father-in-law were gone and now my children were gone. Hearing their voice on the phone didn't help. They were making their own decisions without me. I felt alone. My husband did not understand. He wanted to fix it for me.

"Why don't you want to be with me?" He would ask. I did want to be with him, but I didn't know him anymore. He was the father to my children. He was not my friend, my sister, my mother or my child. He was not the student in my class who I took under my wing. He was the person who ate dinner with us and went on vacation with us. He took me out to eat and paid the bills. He went to church with us and solved the bigger problems. He was no longer my lover. After all, mothers do not have lovers. They have husbands and fathers of their children. I saw my husband as the individual who fixed things around the house. Fathers did not show emotions, so I made the decisions concerning the heart. I expected everyone to take my advice because I was the mother and I knew what was best, or so I thought.

Over the years, I had left him behind to do what fathers do. He worked, came home, mowed the grass and slept. I was never involved in his work and I never asked many questions concerning his day. I was totally wrapped up in our kids and my work. When I stopped working, I turned to the children to fill the empty parts of my day. I would wake at night to listen for them to come home and then I could sleep securely.

Now I look in the mirror and see a very different person looking back at me. She looks familiar but she has no soul. She needs to be with people and she needs to be in charge. What has happened to the feisty woman I use to be?

My sister came to my rescue. In the fall, we took a trip together to Hilton Head and stayed in a condo on the beach. I needed rest from life. Rest from my husband asking me how he could fix things. What was I to tell him? I didn't know what was wrong, so how could I tell him or show him what was happening. We flew to Hilton Head and, while in the air, I had a very strange emotional feeling. I had learned the night before that a good friend of mine, who had cancer, was being hospitalized. She had beaten the odds for several years, and I knew this would be the same type of situation again. She would go in for blood transfusions and be fine in a few days.

Minutes before we landed, I felt uneasy about something and I wanted to cry. Then I started to pray. "God, what is wrong? Are we going to land safely?" I remember questioning. Then thoughts of Susie came to my mind and I prayed for her. I again felt that uncomfortable feeling as I prayed and I knew in my heart that she was gone. I became sad, thinking that I never got to say goodbye. I turned toward the window and peered out into the sky. I could almost feel her presence. I looked into the clouds. "She is gone," I said softly to myself and there was a peace that came over my entire body. I looked out of the plane one more time and I smiled. It was as if Susie was telling me that she was free.

We landed at the smallest airport I had ever seen. We gathered our luggage and headed toward a car waiting to take us to our condo on the beach. As we stopped for lunch, we talked about our past and shared how we were both suffering from feelings that were real, but feelings that we were not sure we wanted to share. We hated some of the things our mom had done in the past and the secrets she made us keep.

We learned that we shared some of the same unhappy moments and regrets. My sister had felt the same way I did concerning the reaction we received from our families. Our husbands and children did not wish to discuss the past and were tired of hearing how we were mistreated. Neither of our current families wanted to hear about our past and what we had lived through.

Feelings for our father were shoved so far in the back of our emotions, that we felt guilty discussing them. Now would be the time. It was just the two of us sitting there crying and sharing together. The silent suffering was over. We pulled up to the condo and pulled our bags up the stairs into the small elevator. We laughed at the number of suitcases we had brought with us. Closing me out of the elevator, my sister pulled on all of her bags and shut the door. I could hear her laughing. I laughed too. I think this was the first time I had laughed in months. Returning to help me get my things into the elevator, she remarked, "We are not used to dragging our own luggage." It was true; we always had our husbands bring our bags to the rooms when we traveled. Now we were on our own.

Tired from our trip, we decided to take a nap and rest before exploring the beach. I tried not to think about home but felt secure knowing that I had my sister with me and together we could figure out what things we needed to unload to make life a better place to be.

Several hours had passed and I woke to a ringing phone. It was my best friend from home. She called to tell me Susie was gone. I asked what time and she gave me the exact time that I was sitting on the plane praying for my friend. I know that God was trying to share that event with me. I also felt that Susie was with me trying to convince me that she was free and happy. I walked outside on the balcony and looked toward the sky. I prayed, "God is there something I need to be free from?" I felt bad that I could not be home for Susie's funeral, but I also knew that I had already felt her presence telling me it was okay. I can not explain why this happened, but it did and I think that when we take the time to listen to God he will give the needed answers.

We talked a lot that trip. We also laughed and cried. I needed time away to fill my cup. I had no responsibilities and I read my devotional book and prayed in quiet places. There is something about the ocean that soothes the soul. The rhythm of the waves pushing into the shore is consistent. Unconsciously, you wait for the next wave to hit the shore. You become aware of the rhythm of your beating heart.

The ocean holds so many mysteries. A creative mind can imagine what is hidden beneath the waters. The ocean represents freedom. It has no boundaries and allows the fish and dolphins to swim and play in the powerful waves.

We must take a lesson from the ocean and learn to find the time for freedom: freedom from the busy life that takes us away from finding out who we are and what we need. I found out on my trip what I needed to know. I learned that change was something I had to accept. Losing a close friend made me think about age and what is to come. It was the first time I realized that I can't stop the change and the next stage of my life.

Just as the hermit crab outgrows his shell and moves on to a bigger shell, I, too, have to move on and find a new shell. I might not want to leave the snug shell that has made me who I am and given me so much pleasure, but the time has come. I must move on.

I suppose everyone is afraid of moving on to the next stage of life. We fear the unknown. I know that I had to try to explain this to my husband and he just did not get it. The more we are together, the more he tells me how lucky we are to have time together, how beautiful I am, and how he just can't stop looking at me. My response is "Where have you been for the last 29 years?"

I want to say, "It's me, dummy: the woman who has always been here, taking care of your children, washing your clothes and fixing your meals. Why are you just now telling me this? I've been on the journey with you walking beside you every step. Why did you not notice me when I was a young mother and a good wife? That's when I wanted you to take notice of my body. Can't you see that I've moved on and time has taken away the best part of me?"

I really don't think that my husband understands that I want to push the clock back. It's not that I don't love him. I love him very much, but I need this space to move into the next stage of my life. I need to feel good in my new skin. I need to see how I can make it as an older woman and a wife. I need time to realize that I am not dying, just getting older. I am having new physical problems that I need to face head on. I need time to realize that I will never again be that young woman I don't see in the mirror anymore. It's over and I need time to learn to love who I have become. Space is scary because I have never taken time and space I need to renew my life and plan for the future. Because of some health problems, I have the space I need. I am trying hard not to look back, but I confess, at times I do push back the curtain and wonder how life slipped by so quickly.

I am free at last for spiritual growth and to explore other interests that I never had time to investigate. I have to focus on my relationship with my husband and not expect him to be the same man I married years ago. Honestly, I don't see him as getting older but I do see the effect of age creeping up on him physically. I don't know what I would do if I lost him. We are together for life. God has a plan for this union, and only God knows when we will be separated.

Take time to enjoy the journey and try to look forward as much as you can. God did not promise that it was going to be easy, but He will help us get where we need to go.

Chapter 8

Do Not Judge

When I owned a Children's Theater, I would go to a discount store to look for props. The woman working in the store had a huge growth hanging off the side of her nose. She was a nice individual, but for the life of me, I could not focus on anything she said. I would stare at her nose. One day I took my assistant with me. We were looking for a used wedding dress. She was showing us what she had in the store and was very helpful in finding a veil to go with the dress. When we walked out of the store, I turned to my assistant and asked, "Did you see her nose?" "Yes," she replied. We talked about it all the way to the theater. We were so focused on her nose! We wondered why she did not want to have it removed.

Then one day when I stopped in to buy something, she started talking to me about raising kids. She asked if I had any children and we began to share. She said that she was raising her children alone. She continued, "With the economy the way it is, I barely make enough money to meet my monthly payments." I said good-bye and, as I drove away, it dawned on me, that she might not have the money to have the growth taken off of her nose. If she is working here, making meager wages, then she might not have insurance. I never saw her again and several months later, the store closed.

I had had plenty of time to get to know this woman. She was always working at the time I was shopping. However, I never wanted to stay any longer than it took to get my items and get out of the store. Physically, she was unpleasant to look at. If I could have taken the time to talk, I am sure she would have loved to share her life with me. She looked like she needed a listening ear, but I was determined it was not going to be mine. I could not get past her physical appearance.

What would Jesus do? In Luke, we see that Jesus heals ten men with leprosy. He did not know these men, but He understood that beyond the skin there was potential for each man to live a fruitful life. With the leprosy, there was no hope for any kind of life. I have no idea if I could have been of any help to this person. What I do know is that I could have been nicer and taken a little more time to be a good listener.

I remember going to a teacher's meeting and getting stuck sitting next to this big, unkempt, loud-mouthed woman. She truly needed a friend. She commented on everything the instructor was saying. I admit I was getting annoyed. I was hoping to move away from her as we got into small groups. To my misfortune, she wanted to be in my group. When she moved her chair, I noticed that she had a big plastic purse and there was something moving in it. Then I saw her talking to her purse. I looked at the teacher sitting next to me and said, "Who is she talking to?" The other teacher started to laugh and replied, "Her dog." I could not believe what I was seeing. She had brought a small poodle with her to class and it was in that small white plastic basket purse. When we were not discussing the topic of the class, she would be communicating with the dog. I was blown away watching this strange woman. I asked her if her dog ever got out. She said that it would sit in there until she took it out. I looked into the purse and there was barely enough room for the dog to move. It never barked but it was certainly entertainment for the women. I have told that story to many people throughout the years. Little did I know that I would run across this woman again in my teaching career.

I was the youngest teacher in my school with a degree in early childhood education. This made me the number one person to be transferred to a kindergarten class that was being put together by our school and another school about half a mile away. I would be teaching a half-day kindergarten in both schools, traveling to the second school at noon. Without a choice, I had the responsibility to put together both classrooms. I started at my school first. I had to clean, put together toys and arrange play centers. Then, about seven at night, I drove to the second school and started on the second classroom. I rang the doorbell at the front of the school and the janitor came and opened the door. I had to explain who I was and why I was there at seven at night. As she was feeling uneasy to admit me into the school, I opened up my trunk and showed her the stack of cut-outs that I had brought to put on my bulletin boards. When she learned that I was the new kindergarten teacher, it all made sense to her.

She showed me to my classroom and I begin to work. I noticed that there was another teacher across the hall, but I didn't have time to socialize. I had much work to do and I wanted to finish before midnight. I finished most of the inside, putting up tables and chairs, along with fun learning centers and rolled out a rug for the reading groups. Just as I was about to take all the things I needed for the bulletin board in the hall, I saw her coming. The conversation went like this:

"Hi. Are you the new kindergarten teacher?" she asked.

"Yes, I am and I will be starting on Monday so I have all this to get together before I leave tonight."

"Well, I am Doris, and I am in the room across the hall."

"Hi, Doris. I am Linda and I am sorry I can't talk right now but I have to keep working."

"Oh, Linda, you're in luck. I am here to help you," she said.

"Thanks, but I am familiar with what I am putting up here and so it will be quicker if I do it myself," I said.

"Okay. I'll keep you company while you work," she said.

"I am usually here all the time and anytime you need anything just come and get me," she continued.

I wanted to ignore her and get my work done so I could get out of there quickly. I really didn't recognize her but I didn't like what I was seeing and the way she was acting. I could tell that she was not the type of person I wanted to spend time with. She kept talking about teachers, and who taught what, and the principal and the lunches. She talked non-stop while I was trying to work. I didn't have to say a word. When I finished, she helped me pick up the scraps and took them into my room.

She surveyed my work and said it looked good. Then she invited me into her room to see her work. Impatiently, I walked across the hall and barely looked in the door. "It looks wonderful. I can tell you put many hours of work into your classroom."

"I work on it all summer," she said.

"All summer?" I questioned.

"Yes, I don't do much, so I spend time over here getting ready for school," she continued.

I thought it was weird but I was tired and so I didn't question her. I gathered my stuff, turned off the light and ran out toward my car.

The next week was busy for me. I was always in a rush to get the kids into the classroom and start my lessons. My main focus after school was to clean up and put out work for the next day. It was a race every day from school to school. Then one day, I stayed after school too long. I was sitting at my desk writing in my lesson plan book. The door opened and in she came. Without a word, she walked over to my piano and started playing the song "Ain't She Sweet." Not only was she playing, she was singing. I looked up from my desk and started laughing. What in the world is this woman doing? I thought. When she finished she continued to play other old songs.

"You know those songs?" she asked.

"Yes, I do," I replied.

"Do you want to sing with me?" she asked.

"No, thank you, I must really be going," I replied.

She helped herself to one of the cookies left over from milk break and said maybe later we could sing together.

I found myself sneaking into my room to avoid Doris. I would leave when I put the kids on the bus. I thought I had it all worked out until one day, as I was arriving at school she was coming from the parking lot.

"Where is your class?" I asked.

"I am on my break so I came out to feed my babies," she replied.

"Babies? What babies?" I asked.

"My dogs, I have my two dogs in the car. I bring them with me everyday," said Doris.

"You bring your dogs?"

"Oh yes! I don't want them to stay home by themselves. I take them out and feed them whenever I get a break."

We walked into school together and she continued to tell me about her babies. I could tell that they were the most important part of her life. Looking at her, I could see that she was not well-groomed, and she didn't wear a ring so I assumed she was not married. I never asked her any questions because I didn't want to hear her go on and on about some kind of nonsense that I could not understand. When she talked, her words slurred. I couldn't tell what age she was, but I knew that she was somewhere over fifty. I gathered that she had been teaching for several years by the way she talked. She taught special education and had about ten to fifteen children in her class. Looking at her classroom, I could tell that it was important that it was decorated like a home. Little doilies were on the window sills. Silk flowers and rugs decorated the empty spaces in the room.

One day, I asked another teacher about Doris. She looked at me and laughed. I could tell by her reaction that there was a story there somewhere.

"Tell me everything, Sara," I requested.

"Here's the scoop," she confessed. "Doris is nuts. She has never married and lives by herself. She has the two dogs that she thinks are her kids. She takes them everywhere. She brings them to school every day. After school she brings them into her classroom."

"What?" I asked, "Tell me more."

"Doris never goes home. She stays here at school until the janitor leaves at night."

"She gets extra food from the lunchroom and puts it in the fridge in the teachers' lounge. Then she eats that for supper. Sometimes she leaves to get something to eat, but mostly she stays here at school and eats."

"You're kidding, me Sara. Why would she do that?" I asked.

"Because the janitor is the only person, beside the dogs, that will talk to her." Replied Sara.

"Oh, I see. You mean she's lonely." I said.

"No, crazy," said Sara.

"She puts that little dog of hers in a little purse and carries it everywhere. She even takes it to meetings with her."

Bingo! I remember her, I thought. This is the crazy woman, at the in-service meeting, who sat beside me five years ago. It was the first time I had put all the pieces together. How could I have not recognized her? Then I shared the story with Sara and she agreed that it was she. Now I had the full story. Poor Doris was so lonely that she needed her dogs with her to talk to. She stayed at school because someone there cared.

Suddenly I started to feel sorry for Doris. She longed to have a friend, but she never learned how to make friends. She was physically unattractive and had a speech problem. How in the world did she ever make it through school to become a teacher? I wondered what happened to her family. Did anyone ever like her? I started to look at her differently.

One day after school, Doris came into my room with her pants unbuttoned. I told her that her pants needed to be buttoned and she remarked, "They are always coming undone." I wondered if her fifth graders noticed and made fun of her.

As she buttoned up her pants, she sat down on the piano bench and started playing *How Great Thy Art*. I started singing as she played. I looked down and she had a smile on her face.

"You know this song, Linda?" She asked.

"Yes, Doris I do. Play it again and sing with me." I said.

When we finished singing, I asked her about her life. I was right: she had never been married. She lived with her mother and father and her father had just passed away. She went on and on about how she took piano lessons and how much her parents loved her. She told me she had an older brother but never saw him. Her life was filled with love that her parents gave her. I suppose, if I could have visited her home, it would have been filled with things from her past. I supposed that her house was just as her parents had decorated it. She talked about her father as if he were still alive and I gathered that she was a daddy's girl.

It made sense that she didn't want to spend time at home if she was living where her father had passed away. Maybe it was sad and lonely there. Being in the school gave her a purpose and a way to be around other people. The dogs were family and she felt needed having them around.

From that day on, I became Doris's friend. I gave her all my leftover cookies from snack time. I would go by her room and tell her good-bye before I left and when she popped into my room, I would take time to listen to her story. Usually it wasn't personal, but she would share something about one of her students or her dogs.

Isn't it amazing the way things change when we learn about the person from the inside out? I didn't have to take Doris out to eat or treat her as my best friend; I just needed to show her kindness. Jesus tells us to be kind to those who torment you. Remember that Jesus searched for people to show them kindness.

Matthew 7: 1-2

"Do not judge, or you too will be judged. For in the same way you judge others you will be judged, and with the measure you use, it will be measured to you."

Chapter 9

How Can We Bloom in Wisdom?

First, we need to define "wisdom." Can we say that it is the ability to know what is good and avoid what is bad? Is wisdom the ability to know several facts about every aspect of life? Is wisdom the ability to recall events and historical dates? Is wisdom having knowledge and using that knowledge to make wise decisions?

I believe that wisdom comes with age and time. We are always telling our children to listen to us because we are older and have already experienced some of the same things they are experiencing now in their young lives. Even failure brings on wisdom. We can try hard to keep failure out of the pathway of our children, but when they make decisions, we have to allow them the freedom to see what the consequences might be. Only when we experience failure first hand, can we see that there are better choices. Hopefully, we will choose more wisely the next time the same situation arises.

Abuse seems to be one of the hardest situations in which to apply wisdom. Children are helpless victims who can't always flee the abuse, but as adults we should protect and give wisdom to children concerning what to do about abuse.

Abuse comes from anger and hurtful words that cause people to feel stupid and insecure about themselves. When we allow these behaviors into our homes and families, we fail to show wisdom and allow this behavior to last a lifetime in the minds and emotions of our loved ones. If abuse is shoved underneath the surface, resentment and anger grow. We try to get beyond the pain but the pain does not go away. Our heart rages against the abuse. With this rage, we can never find joy.

Don't live with abuse. If it means leaving a loved one behind, or losing a job, it is far more important that you face abuse straight on and find the desires of your heart. Please do not abuse your children and try your best to protect them from it. Abuse is a sin and we need to teach our children that God does not want us to be hurt or unhappy.

When children understand that sin is not good then we can teach them what is good. God says that we must show love, truth, happiness, caring, joy, peace, and kindness toward others. When we teach this to our children, they will understand that there is something wrong with the abusive behavior.

We are not doormats just because we are Christians. We will get angry and upset because we are human. We should never allow others to believe that we are not Christians just because we defend ourselves against sinful plans to destroy our confidence. I have seen it in my own family. We have allowed others to take advantage of us because we thought we were turning the other cheek. This is not what God wants us to do. He wants us to be respectful as we teach others that their actions can hurt. Turning the other cheek does not mean getting revenge. It does mean finding ways to show the other person that his action is not godlike or god-honoring.

As Christians, we have the desire to do good. If we continue to allow others to do bad things to us, we are not showing them that being good is desirable. Who wants to do good by allowing others to walk all over us and not telling them that they have hurt us deeply?

Abusers are simple-minded, childish bullies. We have to tell them and show them by example. You might say to the abuser:

- ✓ "For God created me in His own image and if you say hurtful words and do hurtful things to me you are hurting God."

- ✓ "I desire to get even with you, but that is not in God's will."

- ✓ "You are trying to take the joy out of my life, but I will not allow you to steal from me again."

- ✓ "It may be a sinful desire to see you punished, but God sees your wrong and He himself will punish you, for He knows your heart and will deal with your sin."

Acts 1:3 NIV

"After his suffering, he showed himself to these men and gave many convincing proofs that he was alive. He appeared to them over a period of forty days and spoke about the kingdom of God."

We might be suffering here on earth from the things people do and say, but we must remember that there is a better place waiting for us. A whole kingdom where there will be no more sorrow and joy will be flowing from the rivers of life. We will no longer be destroyed, but rather, healed and renewed, brought back to life. All things will be new. This brings joy to my heart as I type it, thinking about all the injustice that I have witnessed from those who try to steal happiness.

"It can't be done." How many times have we heard those words? Negative attitudes steal happiness.

A family member was one of the most negative people I have ever met. When I would start a project and needed help to complete my creative masterpiece, I would hear, "It can't be done." Soon I felt that I could not be creative enough to complete something without a second opinion. I didn't believe in myself anymore.

There will always be some people who go through life with a negative attitude. Most of the time it's "sour grapes." If I can't have it, neither can you. There are people who are jealous of your ideas, lifestyle, and talents and even your looks. Remember, God gives us everything we have. We use it for just a short time here on earth and we leave it here when we die.

We need to know that this is not our home. We are only passing through. It's important to make the most of each day. God gives us each day to enjoy with others. Share happiness and give encouragement whenever possible. Laugh often and make friends with everyone you meet. I am learning when I reach out to others, I am keeping my eyes off of myself. I can't find time to be ungrateful for things God gives me when I am giving attention to those who need someone to care or listen.

Many people who are hurting inside are trying to find others to trust and share personal problems. They may not be ready to express these needs with those close to them. There is hope. God will find ways to put you where He needs you. Remember, each person came into your life for a reason, a season or a lifetime. Maybe you lost a friendship because you moved churches or changed life events. When God feels that this person is the only one that will understand you or listen to you, He will find a way to place that person back into your life. It may be a brief meeting at a store, a phone call or visit. Somehow, God knows what you need and I have seen times when I needed to laugh and He brought me laughter. There were times when I needed to praise Him and He has given me a chance meeting where I could pray with godly people who were believers. God has given me a deeper knowledge of His love. When you understand God's love, you will no longer desire to be with those who are negative. You will desire to be with others that lift you up and as friends together you can share what God has done in your life.

Share in the happiness of your brother. Show concern and give compassion. Spread the love of Jesus and be sincere with your witness. When we give glory to God, He will give us a lesson and help us stand against the enemy. When you doubt who you are and why God has put you here in this world, recognize that Satan is trying to take away happiness. This is a wonderful time to see what the Word of God says about who you are and why He needs you to be His servant. He will show you His purpose and give you the truth about your purpose. Do not believe the lies of others who are trying to tear you away from the Word of God. If only everyone would tell the truth. If only we could trust others. It is not fair that we have to be aware of everyone around us. It would be wonderful and a fairytale world if God had made everyone honest and godly.

Make wise choices when you trust others. Learn who you are. Do not let others tear away your confidence. Remember: It CAN be done.

The truth is God. He will give you wisdom when you pray for it. His wisdom is the greatest gift you can pass on to your loved ones. Be wise and listen to God's words.

Chapter 10

The Oz Complex

Most of us have seen the movie "The Wizard of Oz" many times. I remember watching it as a child and being afraid to watch the whole movie. Even though it scared me, I still wanted to sit there for the good parts. I loved the music and the dancing. As I got older, I must have watched it over twenty times and still I never really understood the meaning behind the movie. Years later, I realized that I had not seen the entire movie from beginning to the end. I had left the room or hidden my face when the storm started or the witch jumped out and when the monkeys chased Dorothy and her friends.

One day I remember listening to someone tell about the making of the movie and the way they had to dress in those monkey suits. I looked at the person and said, "What monkeys?" Now everyone was looking at me as if I had a bad hair day and didn't know it.

One person in the group said, "You have seen the movie, haven't you?"

"Yes, of course, I have. Many times."

"You don't remember the monkeys?"

"No," I said as I thought back about the movie.

"Next time it comes on I will call you and you make sure you watch it," she laughed.

It wasn't too long after that when I learned that the show would be on TV. I decided to sit down, watch the whole movie and only leave during the commercials. My friend was right. There were monkeys in the movie. I was an adult then and I had to laugh, wondering why I left the room or was afraid of the movie. It was also the first time I understood the movie. To refresh your memory, each character (Scarecrow, Tinman and Lion) lacked certain attributes that kept them from being a complete individual. They go with Dorothy to meet the Wizard who will fix them. They were looking for courage, love, and brains. Dorothy was looking for knowledge to find her way home.

After completing tasks to prove their worthiness, they realize that the Wizard could not help them. They already had all these things but had never been told or shown how to use them. I still wasn't sure where the monkeys fit in. Then I got it. The monkeys were controlled by the Witch to show she had power. Now isn't that like Satan? He has his own monkeys that he sends toward us to scare us and make us think he has power over God. The monkeys were the puppets controlled by the Witch.

When we don't pay attention to the good things and good people who surround us, we can become puppets of Satan. I know this sounds bizarre, but it can happen in a blink of an eye, especially to your children. It seems like only yesterday that I was controlling what my children were watching on TV, who they went out with, and where they were going. I took them to church and taught them what God thinks is good and before I could turn around twice and click my heels, my children were grown and gone. Now they are in the world with all of Satan's monkeys. Satan's monkeys are surrounding them daily whispering in their ears. Satan's monkeys are telling our young adults and children that what they learned in church and at home is not what everyone else believes. I can just hear the Witch screaming in the air with her high pitched crackling voice, "Go ahead and do it, it's not a sin anymore." Then she gives a laugh as if she has just spread a bag of sin dust over the world. "Go for it!" she says, as she freely flies around the young people who have stopped reading the Word and attending church. "It's okay. You don't have to go to church to be a good Christian."

The witch never tells the truth. She does not explain that if you want to be a better Christian, you will desire to drink in the gospel and be with others who have the same desire.

The last part of the story is all about the Wizard. He is the big bad scary voice that controls the people of the village. Do you have friends like the Wizard? I am sure we each have one or maybe two.

The other day my husband and I were in the car and I had a flashback about some of the friends we used to have. One couple in our church was so much fun. We had traveled together to church events and we spent time together at each of our houses. I was always one of those people that would make jokes and make people laugh. I took nothing seriously even if people teased or said things about me. I could dish it out and take it back. All statements were in jest. Then I began to notice the comments were no longer appreciated as group humor. It all pointed toward something I had said or done. For a while, I said nothing and let it slide. Then one day I noticed that one woman was directing her harsh statements to me personally to see what I would say or how I would react. I remember it like it was yesterday.

"Why do you feel that you have to dress up or wear a loud blouse when the rest of us are dressed in jeans?"

I was the only person she knew standing there so I looked at her and said, "What are you talking about?"

"You always want to be noticed, don't you?" She continued.

"No," I answered, "I liked this blouse and thought it would be comfortable to wear. It has sleeves that are thin and not too hot. Why do you care what I wear?"

She shook her head and walked away in a huff. Later, on another trip as we all gathered to go eat, she attacked me again.

"Who is wearing that sickening perfume?" She boldly turned to me and smelled in my direction. "What is that smell?" she continued.

"I like that smell," someone else remarked not realizing that she was trying to criticize my taste for perfume.

"Just walk away from me," she continued as she passed me on the sidewalk.

Each time we were together, I could see that she was not enjoying my company. Anytime she could make a smart remark, she would direct it to me. Others in the group did not see that she was picking me to death. She enjoyed building herself up. She was always talking about her job and being boss over so many people. She didn't have a college education but was lucky enough to be in charge of her firm. Obviously, she was good at her job.

Regardless of her insults, I continued to ignore her and had fun with the group. Then one day I noticed that my husband and I were totally removed from the group on purpose. We were late coming to a party and when we arrived, they were playing a game. She looked up at both of us and said, "You can't play. We have already started."

That was fine with us, but when the next game started, she told us to sit at another table.

"I don't want them on my team," she announced. "Neither one of them ever go to concerts or know about current events. I want to win." She continued with a laugh that didn't go over well with the rest of the group.

The host was generous and explained that she was just teasing. I knew that she was not teasing by the sound of her voice. She had scolded me before and I knew that she was being rude.

Soon the group rejected us. She had so much power over the group of couples that she insisted we not be invited to a party or dinner. She had the most wonderful husband. He enjoyed the Lord and being with Christian people. We could discuss our faith and God. He was more considerate with people. I could not understand why he did not see the angry, hateful side of his wife. She even yelled at him for no reason.

I remember going to church and I went up the steps to sit in the balcony. I was not aware that it was saved for members who were her groupies.

"No, you can't sit here. This is for Alice and for my friends." She began to name members in her group. "We always sit up here together."

That was the last straw. We left and went down front to find an empty seat.

I allowed her to tear me apart. She hurt my feelings and I allowed her to control where I sat, what I wore to church, and to whom I could speak. If I saw her coming in my direction, I would say, "Hi," but nothing else. She would make sure she bragged about her children, her job, and her husband and, of course, everything she owned was much better than anything I owned. She would give me the latest news even though I had already heard it. I was reluctant to share anything with her. I never told her anything unless she asked.

If I wore something that was a designer brand, I made a special point to set it down or cover it over so she would not remark on what I was carrying or wearing. I was so uncomfortable around her. I dreaded running into her at church. I wracked my brain trying to figure out why this girl did not like me. "Have I done something to her?" I wondered.

This so-called friend, Trish (not her real name), was a client of my husband's. She was nice when she was in the office, but a different person when she needed my husband's services. She had no reason to hate us or anything we had done. I was much older than she and we had nothing in common but the church. Her children were not in my classes. My husband and I were frequently asked to host parties because we had room for sit-down dinners for large groups. Trish was always included. I never understood why she was rude to me.

 I prayed about it all the time. I did not ask her why she hated me. I later wished I had approached her and discussed the situation. I believe it was my past that kept me silent. After facing bullies in youth groups and school, I just wanted to be quiet and stay out of her way. Maybe that was a good choice because we couldn't be happier than we are now. My son went to a private Baptist school in the sixth grade. Even though we were not Baptist, we wanted to support him and so we changed churches. It was the best thing we could have done. God has blessed us in everything we do for Him and His people. Our friends are truly Christians that enjoy serving the Lord.

In my teen years in youth group, I worked for the Lord. I went on mission trips and played the piano for church. I dated one of the most eligible young men at the church. I had no idea that a group of girls would egg my car because they were jealous of me. I didn't even know the girls that well. They were much younger and we had no reason to be in the same class or youth group. It wasn't until I got bladder cancer that they all came to me and apologized to me for their actions. It turned out that they were jealous.

It has been fifteen years since we attended the old church. I was thinking about this woman and the way I had allowed her to take over my life and self-confidence. My husband listened to me as I remembered some of the remarks she spat at me. He started laughing and said, "You know, honey, she must have been very insecure to treat you that way."

"What are you talking about?" I replied.

"People who put other people down are very insecure in their skin."

"How so?" I asked.

"Well, you might think she was scary, but she was jealous. Think about it. She never went to college, she lived in a small house, she was always overweight, she didn't have money for parties or money to pay her bills on time. She was always trying to make herself look good in your eyes."

"So you think she was jealous of ME?" I asked.

"Of course. You could teach choir, the kids church and do things she could not do," he answered.

"Why in the world would she be jealous of me?" I kept repeating.

"Honey, you are good looking. You have a beautiful home. You have many friends, and you have a handsome husband, who makes more money than her husband."

"I never thought of it that way," I said. "Just remember who you are and don't get so cocky, Honey. God doesn't care who we are or what we have."

"I know. I was just kidding. But it's true, honey," he replied. "Think about the rude people you have dealt with in business and other places. Doesn't this sound familiar? People who are insecure have to make themselves look good even at the expense of others."

On the way home I got to thinking about what he was saying. Why didn't I think of that? Why did I let this girl talk about me and shun me? Then I thought about the Wizard in the story. He was nothing without his loudspeaker and loud deep voice.

As long as the wizard was behind the green curtain, he was scary and he could pretend that he was mighty and had special powers. He could do magic and fix any problem. The people believed in him and did not want to face him because he was almighty and powerful. He was so convinced that he could fool all the people, that he had convinced himself that he was really the Wizard. It was not until Dorothy pulled back the curtain and saw a small, bent over, old man that people knew the real secret he was hiding.

He was not a wizard or did not posses any powers. He was just a person like the others. It was a huge disappointment to him that others could see who he really was. This is when the Good Witch Glenda came and informed the travelers that they already possessed the things they were hoping to get from the Wizard.

The Lion had to believe in himself so others would respect him and believe in him. The Tin Man had to show compassion for others so he and everyone who met him knew that he was a man with a heart. The Scarecrow had a brain but was never allowed to use it. He waited for instruction from the farmer to chase away the birds. He didn't realize that he could think on his own. He was out there in the field everyday and he knew when to chase away the birds. He knew better than the farmer, but he did not know that he could make decisions on his own and use his own techniques to chase the birds.

Dorothy had on magic shoes but didn't realize they were magic. She could have been home at any time, but she had to be on the journey to have an opportunity to meet her friends. Together they gave each other the confidence to visit the Wizard. Without Dorothy's involvement and encouragement, I am sure they would never have changed. Dorothy was the strong person who had the faith to continue.

I compare Dorothy to the Christian who is also taking the journey but sees along the way that others are discouraged and give up. Dorothy knows what her goal in life is and she is determined to get what she wants. When the others want to turn back, she keeps them focused on the prize and the desirable things that will happen if each one continues to press forward.

Do you have a Wizard friend? Do you listen to what they tell you and do what they say is important? If you do, get rid of them right now. God is the only one you should believe. Read His Word and listen to what He is telling you. Don't let others take away your magic. Surround yourself with strong, positive friends who believe in you and will encourage your journey.

We have no idea how much power exists in our being. We are appreciated when we say something positive, listen to those who are hurting, do for others and give to those in need. These are important parts of our personality that we should cultivate. Focus on the positive and not the negative. I can't stress it enough.

In the Bible, Jesus talks about the sheep and the Shepherd. Sinners are sheep, wildly roaming over the mountaintop without a Shepherd. They look for food on rocks instead of grassy areas. They follow each other aimlessly, not finding a stream of water or a safe place to rest. Without the safety of the Lord, or Shepherd, they will not survive. Jesus is our Shepherd and I believe that Dorothy represents the Shepherd in this story.

I should never have allowed my Wizard friend to tear me apart and put me down. I have learned not to allow someone to steal my happiness. If I do something wrong, I will know because of my relationship with God. If someone makes fun of me or calls me names, I don't take it to heart. I have loving friends with whom I can share my problems and they will help me find the answers in God's Word. Remember, when all else fails, ask yourself, "What would Jesus do?"

When we attempt to take the ownership of our personal pain or deficiencies, God will respond and do His part. He will bring healing. It might take us a long time to travel the road to peace and contentment, but there is Someone who hears our hearts and knows our unspoken thoughts. His name is Jesus. I believe that was the role of Glenda. She opened the eyes of the travelers and when they knew the truth, they were free.

There will come a day when we will no longer suffer daily problems. Praise God, we will be in Heaven, happy and comfortable.

Chapter 11

Expressing Your Desire to

Heal Your Wounded Spirit

Before we can heal, we have to admit to ourselves that we are sick and need help. Sometimes it takes more than a Band-Aid.

So many times, we stick our heads in the sand hoping that others won't see us and get to know who we really are. With your head in the sand, you must remember that the rest of your body is sticking out. You might not think anyone sees your pain, but it becomes obvious when you avoid the people you love and refuse to face the truth.

One of my favorite books is *Balcony People* by Joyce Landorf Heatherley. In the book, she talks about people who have been given massive doses of rejection. This is not something we can avoid. Each one of us will face rejection several times in our life. This is a major component that wounds the spirit. When we feel we are rejected by the ones we love, we feel the cut deep into our spirit. As I've stated many times in this book, it is important that we develop a good self image early in life. If we are called names, or given the idea that we are not accepted by a parent or loved one, then we must start back at the beginning of life where the problem began.

It's hard to look back. I try everyday to keep the past in the past. Sometimes, when we live in the past, we miss the future. There are too many people blaming their present failures on the past. It is important to see why people keep going backward to understand where they are going.

I come from a divorced home. I remember being doted on and loved and kissed everyday. Then one day, I can't remember at what age or when, all the cute little things I did were no longer cute. I was a quiet child. I remember my parents yelling and fighting many nights. Somehow, I think I took responsibility for their dying marriage. The love and kisses stopped and the cute little things were never again noticed. Of course, I had no role in their divorce. I was part of the problem because child support and visitation needed to be addressed. The connection between the lack of hugs and kisses was the lack of my mother's concentration on her children, and lack of a parent around to share in the confirmation that I was special, cute and loved.

I tell you this story to show how crazy our thoughts become when we do not receive positive affirmation from our parents. Affirmation is very important in childhood and needs to continue throughout life. Affirmation brings happiness and smiles. We will never understand affirmation until we understand rejection. Learning about the people around you will help you understand why they are needy and need to be affirmed.

The dictionary defines rejection as broken, shattered, defeated, not included, humiliated, shunned, and forgotten. The effects of rejection can take many forms.

- ❖ Rejection makes people recoil from society.

- ❖ Rejection takes away creativity and adventurousness.

- ❖ Rejection makes it difficult to make new friends.

- ❖ Rejection takes away independence.

- ❖ Rejection makes sharing difficult.

- ❖ Rejection makes completing projects difficult.

- ❖ Rejection makes life changes agonizing.

- ❖ Rejection makes leadership impossible.

People who have been rejected are consistently hiding. They spend their whole life afraid that there will be more rejection and they have no idea how to handle the feelings that come with rejection. These people do not see the good things in their personality. They only see the bumps in the road and the scars that others have placed there with insults and name-calling.

Anger is one of the signs of rejection. I have seen children who come to school with anger, ready to start a fight for no reason. Putting this child in time out or other punishment only brings out more anger. The most important thing to do with this child is to sit down and talk. Let them know they look angry and that it is okay. Everyone gets angry. Then according to the age, give the child a crayon and paper and tell him to draw or write some things that make him angry. This way, the teacher has confirmed that she understands his feelings. Now this child has a friend to confide in.

There are many forms of affirmation: **g**iving hugs, listening, saying positive things about physical behavior, showing positive behavior, saying "I need you" and "you are important" and showing concern. All of these behaviors give validity.

Joyce Heatherley tells us in her book that we, as Christians, need to look for people who will affirm us. She separates the negative people and positive people by calling them basement and balcony people. Isn't that a wonderful way of letting us know that we should be supportive and not be negative?

The basements in our houses are usually dark, with no windows, and hold things that are not necessary to live. Some basements are full of mold and smell musty. Basements hold our pipes, water heaters and electrical boxes, things not desirable on the main floor where people can sit and enjoy entertaining guests.

The balcony is above the main floor and usually has a view and a place to sit outside of the house. Big colonial homes had huge balconies where there was fresh air. The balconies gave a feeling of freedom from inside restraints. Often eminent people stood on balconies to give speeches so everyone could hear important information. Not all houses had balconies. The most affluent citizens had houses with a balcony for viewing the property they owned.

Mrs. Heatherly gives a good method for choosing friends. Paraphrased here, it is a simple explanation for those who are trying to heal wounded spirits and make new friends.

- ✓ Choose friends that will affirm you.

- ✓ Make a list of things that make you feel rejected. Make a list of things that hurt you.

- ✓ Stay away from situations where there are people that make you feel sad or uncomfortable. (Those going through depression, divorce, or family problems.)

- ✓ Stay away from basement people, if possible.

- ✓ Make a list of balcony people: those who love you and support you no matter what you go through.

Balcony people do not keep score and never compete with each other. They are full of love and respect. They enjoy delighting each other with advice and solutions. Balcony people love from the heart, knowing God is their support and reason for their support of others. Balcony people know who you are and they do not judge you, but support you through the rough times even when you make mistakes.

Don't be afraid to call your balcony people and let them know that you need them. If we don't call upon the people we trust, we will surely fall back into rejection and listening to basement people. When we call upon our balcony people, we start to realize that maybe the situation is not as bad as we thought.

Yes, we can always find someone who is worse off than we are, but why settle for just existing? We want to know that we are affirmed. We need to believe that God has released us from the basement and put balcony people in our lives for a reason.

One of my biggest failures in friendship is listening. I try, but I always somehow seem to interject some personal experience into their story that brings the conversation back to me. I have to stop and remember that my role in being a balcony person is to listen to my friends. I don't have to give advice or solve the problem. Sometimes people just need you to listen and show concern. You can always ask, "How can I help you?" Just be sure that you listen and pray with the person who has chosen you as their balcony person.

If you do not agree with the person you are consulting with, then ask if you can pray with them. Use the Bible to show where there may be a problem if certain choices are made without thinking of the consequences. Remember to show Christian love as in the New Testament. It is important to read Romans, John, James and Corinthians.

Ephesians: 4:2

"Be patient with each other, making allowance for each other's fault because of your love."

1 Corinthians: 16:14

"Whatever you do, do it with kindness and love."

I know Paul was a balcony person and I think we can learn much from his teachings and his faith.

Here's an exercise to bring things into focus. Make a list of your balcony people. Don't forget to list family members. List the reasons you think your spirit has been broken. Who do you hold responsible?

The important part of this exercise is to stop and seek solitude and healing with prayer and the Word. We have to be willing to accept the presence of the Spirit to find comfort. I call comfort a peace of mind that sometimes helps me to stop worrying about things over which I have no control.

If you have ever lost a loved one, you go through many phases. The last realistic phase is peace. We must realize that the deceased has no life, will not be coming home, and the only way we can make it through each day is to pray. God is the only person who knows your heart and He is the only one that can help you face reality. He is our hope and He is the only person who can change our attitude toward life. If we ask Him, He can show us our purpose for being here on earth.

When we are born, Jesus has already planted in our mother's womb the seed that will make up personality, physical features, and the role to be played in society. God has planned everything about you. This does not mean that we will grow up and follow His path that He has carved out. We will not take off like a racecar to be the person God wants us to be. The reason is because we are all born with free will. We are born into a hostile world and without proper guidance, we could become sinful. We are followers of others who are sinners. Until we learn that there is a proper way to do things and say things, we will continue to follow our own feelings, thoughts and behave like others who are exploring the untamed world.

Think of a racehorse that is born in the spring. It stands and walks right away. It nurses from its mother and then learns to eat hay or grass. Untrained, it can only play in the field and exercise with other horses. If this horse were bred to be a runner, it will have to be trained. There will be several steps to follow, as the trainer will work daily to produce a good racehorse. The horse will learn to run faster each day and the trainer will continue to mold the horse to develop strength. If this is a Kentucky Derby contender, it was likely bred from other winners, and received the proper genetics it will need to win the race.

I believe that God gives each one of us the proper genetics to become winners. Like the horse, we need the training, the love and the guidance that only God can give us. When God gives you a talent, He will introduce you to the elements that are needed to show you that you are special. When we fail to follow God's directions, we may take years to find our purpose in life and the happiness that comes with it.

When you do have that direction, you immediately know that with faith you can accomplish the goals that make you feel important and happy. This will give you peace, knowing you are a child of God and He is guiding your life always.

Chapter 12

Learning to Trust

Like a wounded cat or dog, we look at people differently than we did before our injuries. Most wounded spirits back away from authority figures, knowing instantly that authority figures are somehow going to make you feel insecure. Trusting means you have to express feelings, whether they are joy, disappointment, or happiness.

Wounded spirits cannot keep relationships for long periods because it is hard to let go and learn to love. The risk of being hurt again is too great for those who have spent a lifetime suffering because of others.

Wounded spirits believe that they are the problem. They are always trying to please others. They want and need love but have problems with intimacy. Wounded spirits have problems making decisions. It is not unusual for the wounded spirit to ask several people's advice before making a decision. Making simple decisions like grocery shopping becomes difficult because they want to make sure that their decisions are pleasing to those they are shopping for. Wounded spirits sometimes give up and refuse to face responsibilities like paying bills. They are afraid they may pay the wrong amount or send it to the wrong place. Being wrong is devastating to a person who has been punished continuously for making wrong decisions. Learning to trust that they are making the right decision usually comes with therapy.

People who have been wounded find it important to take care of others instead of themselves. If they learn to honor themselves, then they have to accept their behavior and love themselves. If they are pleasing others, they are not looking inward but outward. Acceptance is coming from outside and they need to be needed by others even if it is for a short time. Unfortunately, people will continue to take advantage of people who show kindness and the hurting will develop from any relationship when there is all taking and no giving.

How many times have we seen couples where one spouse will be the taker and no matter what is said or done, the giver will not leave the marriage because they are needed? This spouse never sees the whole picture. As long as the wounded spirit feels needed, they feel that everything is okay in the marriage. Sadly, many spouses want the other spouse to believe that they cannot exist without him or her. After several years of being told, "You are nothing without me," you begin to believe that you have no value.

It is important to learn to trust yourself so you can start caring about yourself. We need to know that we can solve problems. It is important to find confidence to speak out against what we do and do not believe. We have a right to share our feelings no matter what others may say to discourage us. Everyone needs to be free to express feelings of hurt, rejection, and frustration. Expressing your emotions tells others that you have a voice and you are not going to let others control you physically, mentally, or emotionally.

Look at the animal kingdom; it is always the weaker animal that is easy prey for the much stronger lion or tiger. By showing strong characteristics in your personality, you are letting others know:

> ➤ You have a voice and you are a person that will not tolerate behavior that is hurtful or undesirable.

> ➤ You no longer agree with the crowd or person that walks all over people. The people that are not showing independence are people who are afraid to fight for their right to make decisions.

There are so many people who have accepted bad and undesirable behavior for so long, they believe they deserve to be treated this way. There are also some who believe they are doing the godly thing by allowing others to take advantage of them. When others observe this, then it becomes the norm.

I have a relationship with a wonderful person who is kind, understanding and more than giving. She is willing to give to anyone who gives her a sad story. She believes that most of the people in the world are good and mean what they say. Because of this type of thinking, she has lost the respect of her fellow employees and friends. They ask for advances on checks and give sad stories that allow them a day off with pay. Soon everyone in her inner circle starts to believe they can take advantage of her.

Over the years, she has lost not only respect, but also money that would have helped her build her business. Now she is at retirement age and she will never be able to be secure in her retirement. Money has been stolen from her. When people saw that she was not willing to question or take action against an assistant that took advantage of her kindness, she became an easy target. The staff felt that she would not mind if they took a dozen stamps from the office, or borrowed the office sweeper, or stole free coffee cups that were given to the boss. Everyone said, "I didn't think you would mind."

My friend never gave herself a voice in the office and everyone thought they could take whatever they wanted because the boss would not dare create problems or hurt anyone's feelings.

This is always the way embezzlement happens. Right under the boss's nose, people lie and tell the boss what he or she wants to hear. This is called "the set up." When you allow others to have special privileges, they will test you. The boss wants to be the good person and so agrees, and in return, the employee will do favors for the boss. Soon there is a trust built between the two and no matter who goes against the employee, the boss is not going to believe the others in the office. This being the case, others will continue the same tricks, asking for favors and having them granted.

I have known several offices where the main secretary has taken advantage of a good, kind person by babysitting the boss' children, or running errands outside of work.

Facing difficult clients so the boss can continue working on projects is one of the biggest favors that secretaries do. Because she does these favors, she feels like she deserves the money.

When we start to trust individuals, we do not expect them to always be true to their word. Ask questions and review work ethics. Make sure they respect their job and you. You can set yourself up for failure when you start trusting everyone. Just because people tell you they are Christian, do not automatically believe they are honest and trustworthy. People will tell you what they think you want to hear.

Set boundaries and make sure that they respect the boundaries. This also goes for your friends and family members.

➢ Do not accept anyone who lies.

➢ Do not accept irresponsible behavior.

➢ Do not allow anyone to speak disrespectfully.

➢ Do not lie for anyone.

Please remember the rules and do not change them or you are allowing someone to make you feel guilty.

If you are a wounded spirit, you must learn to take responsibility in a leadership role. Trust your gut feeling and pray about your decisions. Don't let others control you or condemn you. Remember that you are a good person and do not allow others to take self-confidence and trust away.

II Timothy 1:7 (New Scofield Reference Bible)

"For God hath not given us the spirit of fear, but of power, and of love and of a sound mind."

Chapter 13

Hope

How can we possibly go on without believing that there is hope for a better future? Some people who have suffered day after day and year after year believe that they are doomed to a life without hope. This is certainly not the case. When you believe in Christ, you can find hope in His Word. Hope depends on how each individual anticipates the future. We must try to be positive and know that nothing is impossible with God.

Hope will help you make decisions. Hope will give you self-confidence. Hope will help you learn to love yourself. Hope will put a smile on your face when things around you are bad or uncertain. You must believe that hope is in your future and, with help from those who love you and the love of Jesus Christ, there will be a way to solve the problems.

Sharon was an only child. She was the pride of her family, which included her parents and a grandmother and grandfather. Everything she did was noticed and praised. She thought she was the best at everything she did. When she started school, she realized that she was in competition with other children who were better ball players, skaters, runners, and dancers. This upset Sharon because she never had to compete with anyone. Her early years in school were not happy ones. She made friends with children that she knew she could control. There were girls that she could beat in a race and girls that she could outdance. As she got older, she realized that being the best was not going to happen in high school. There were students who were smarter than she was in all academic areas. Sharon had to search harder to find friends who were not interested in school. These friends would never be on the honor roll. They were friends with parents who didn't care where they went on weekends. She had friends whose parents didn't care who their children's friends were. It was not the group that Sharon's family would be happy entertaining at their home.

As Sharon continued her life, she soon met a man that she thought was her knight in shining armor and married him right out of high school. He came from a large family and they liked to drink and party. Sharon took on the lifestyle of her new family. She tried to fit in with all her sisters-in-law and soon she found out that the family was not as caring as her family. She found herself arguing with her mother over her weekend drinking and hanging out at bars with her husband and his friends.

Now Sharon was thinking that the life she had was not real. The only way to celebrate with those who loved her was to buy a keg of beer and get drunk. Soon she was seeing another side of life. Her husband was going out drinking without her and making excuses when he came home late. Sharon was working overtime to make ends meet and her husband was asking for money to satisfy his needs. He was being encouraged by friends to go back to school and lose Sharon.

One night, as Sharon walked into the house after working a ten-hour shift, her husband informed her that he wanted to move on. He told her that he wanted to get a better job and the only way to do that was to go back to school and work part time.

"I know we could make it on your salary and mine, but who knows how long your job will allow you to work overtime," he explained. "I can support myself and take one or two classes a semester and will be able to graduate sometime in the next three years. I wouldn't want you to be strapped because of me. I just love you too much."

What a lie, thought Sharon.

Sharon knew that the late night drinking was not with buddies. She had heard that he was seeing some girl from the bar. What he really wanted was to move in with his girlfriend, pay no rent or bills and use all of his money for school. How dumb could this girl be, thought Sharon? Glen only loves himself.

Sharon's life had just fallen apart. Now she had to face her mother and father. That was the hardest part of this broken relationship. Sharon told her parents, but turned to her friends for advice instead of her parents. She continued to hang out at bars and drink every chance she could. She wanted to prove to her husband, Glen, that she was fun and desirable. Soon she was attracted to another man. He was newly divorced and seemed to share the same feelings and problems that she had. Sharon was meeting him weekly and inviting him over for meals. He did not love Sharon but knew that she was a good person and would accept his problem of alcoholism. Sharon had no idea that Kevin had a problem. They partied on the weekends and Kevin would pass out on the couch when they arrived home. Soon Kevin asked Sharon to marry him. He gave her every reason he could think of to show that they were made to be together. He told her that he loved her and he would take good care of her. Sharon fell for it hook, line, and sinker. Kevin had a good job and made good money. This would mean that Sharon would not have to work overtime.

A year after they met, Sharon and Kevin were married. Again, her mother and father were not sure that she made the right decision. Kevin did not like to be around people, especially her parents. He was sure that they would discover his problem. It was hard for him to go to family functions without beer and liquor. Kevin soon opted out of family events and spent time at home watching ball games and drinking beer. He never wanted to do anything with Sharon. He needed to drink, and would beg Sharon to go to the bar with him, like the old times. To spend time with her husband, Sharon went with Kevin to their favorite bar.

They would drink and party with friends, often having friends drive them home. Sharon became convinced that there was not going to be a life with Kevin until he learned to stop drinking. She also noticed that she wanted a drink in the middle of the day. Secretly, she was worried about the two of them.

When she approached Kevin about the addiction, he became very angry. She would prepare meals for him at night and he would not come home. One time he disappeared for a week. Sharon could not believe that she had again gotten into a marriage that would end up in divorce. When Kevin came home, he would always start an argument. They would call each other names and Sharon would leave and spend time with her family. She waited months before she was able to tell them that she was thinking about getting a divorce. Kevin sent her divorce papers and she signed them. Kevin left town and Sharon never heard from him again.

Sharon felt like a failure and could not see any hope of happiness in her future. How could this be happening to her? What had she done wrong? The only place she knew she could find peace was back at the bar with her drinking friends. She knew that her family would only lecture her and tell her that she was no good. Sharon set out to spend time with her old friends. Drinking seemed to ease the pain of losing Kevin and Glen. She had no self-worth and did not know that she was one of God's children. She had never heard that God made her for a reason and, therefore, she lost all hope.

The friends at the bar convinced her that she would find someone else who would love her and marry her. They wanted her to always party with them, and they never gave her encouragement for life without alcohol. They never told her that she had become dependent on this substance for happiness. They did not give her hope or encourage her to look at her lifestyle. It took something else to open up Sharon's broken heart and see that there was more to life than partying.

Sharon's life began to change as she stood at the foot of her mother's casket. She had never been close to her mother. She never took care of her mother and she never told her mother why she had failed marriages. Her father was weeping uncontrollably as she passed her arm around his waist and kissed him on the cheek. It was apparent they had something special that she would never understand. She had given up all hope of a relationship. Where had she gone wrong? How could she give her father the hope he needed when she had no hope of her own?

Later that week, Sharon and her father were going through the contents of the house.

"Dad, I just want to say that I promise to come by once a week to see you," said Sharon.

"Thanks baby, but I'll be just fine. You have your own life," her father answered.

"I want to be closer to you. I know I was not the best daughter. I can't make it up to mom, but I can try to make it up to you."

"I will always love you, Sharon. You do not need to make up anything to me. I only hope that you find the same love and happiness that Mom and I had. We worked together to make life easier for each other. It's like God knew we needed each other and He put us together."

It was the first time Sharon had ever heard her father talk about God. It shocked her. She thought about what he said and knew that he was on to something. Maybe God did have something to do with them being together.

"Could this be true?" Sharon questioned as she folded up her mother's nightgowns and placed them in the box for the Community Chest.

That night, Sharon was tempted to go to the bar and visit with her friends, but instead she sat on the couch with a big cup of coffee. She was remembering everything the minister had said about God and heaven. She wanted to know if there really was hope of seeing her mother again in Heaven. She had never prayed and didn't know much about church and the Bible. For some reason she was wishing for a Bible to see what God was saying about Heaven and hope. Yes, hope. That is what she needed now. Was she going to get a second chance at life? Confused and concerned, Sharon turned off the light and fell asleep on the couch.

A few weeks, later Sharon got a visit from a friend that she had not seen for a long time. While Sharon was typing at her desk, she looked up and noticed that someone was standing in front of her.

"Amanda Stewart, what in the world are you doing here?"

"Sharon, I was hoping that you were going to be working today," said Amanda. "I have been thinking about you since I heard about your mother. I am so sorry I didn't get to the funeral home but I have been out of town."

"That's okay, Amanda," said Sharon. "It was one of the hardest things I have ever had to face."

"I am sure it was. Here, I brought you something," said Amanda as she handed her a present.

Sharon took the present and opened it. "You didn't have to get me anything, Amanda. A phone call would have been just fine."

"Well, the Lord put in my heart to give you this Bible," said Amanda. "I know you don't go to church anywhere and we have never really talked about religion, but remember that it doesn't matter where you go to church. You just need to believe in God. I was given a Study Bible when my grandmother died and I can understand it because each verse is explained at the bottom of the page."

Amanda opened up the Bible and showed Sharon how she used the Bible.

"You're not trying to get me to go to church, are you Amanda?" asked Sharon.

"No! I am just trying to show you how I was encouraged to continue living after I felt that the life had been snuffed out of me. My grandmother raised me and she was the mother I never had. This Bible gave me hope."

"Hope?" This was the very thing that Sharon was looking for. Why had Amanda used that word? Why had she shown up at work when Sharon had not seen her for years?

"Sharon, we used to be friends when I worked here. I am sorry we did not keep in touch, but I still consider you one of my good friends. It's my fault for not calling but you would not believe how crazy my life has been," said Amanda.

Sharon was thinking to herself: No, you would not believe my life, either. Sharon took the Bible and held it close to her chest. "Thank You Amanda. I have missed all of our fun times. Maybe we can go to lunch one day and catch up."

Before Amanda left the office, she gave Sharon a hug. They made plans to meet for lunch and Sharon was looking forward to going home and reading her new Bible.

Sharon did find hope in God's word. She talked to her best friend Karen about the visit and the Bible. Karen was glad that someone had given Sharon a piece of hope. She had been sad to see Sharon so depressed and hopeless. Nothing Karen could say would make Sharon feel better. If Sharon could find hope in a Bible, maybe she needed to find a study Bible for herself.

Today, several years later, Sharon has learned that true love comes from people that respect you and your values. It took some time and counseling, but Sharon learned that living alone was not a bad thing. She has time for herself and she has learned to love who she really is. She no longer depends on alcohol or other people for happiness. Sharon met a Christian friend in group counseling. After many weeks of learning about God's will and reading her Study Bible, Sharon became a member of her friend's church and was baptized.

Sharon tells everyone that she does not want to rush into a relationship until she finds the right person.

"I have found the hope that I always needed," says Sharon.

Sharon is involved with singles groups in church and volunteers in Christian activities. She has given hope to others that have given up on life. Her hope is in the love of Christ who died to take away our sins so we can have everlasting life. Sharon will tell you that she knows for sure that she will one day go to Heaven. Until then, she continues to witness to others who are not believers. Her definition of hope is <u>H</u>elping <u>O</u>thers <u>P</u>repare for <u>E</u>ternity.

Chapter 14

Joy

There is no greater joy than when you hold your newborn baby in your arms for the first time. If you are a parent, think about that day and that time. I can remember sitting in my new rocker in my baby's room waiting for my delivery day. I was nine months pregnant and so excited to meet this little baby who had been growing inside of me. I didn't know if it was a boy or girl but I did know it was mine. It was a gift that God gave my husband and me and no one would enjoy that excitement as we would. We had names picked out and a room ready to receive the newest member of our family. A family of my own! I was rejoicing knowing that I would soon have a family with a father, mother and, now, a baby. I did not grow up with my father in my home, so I was excited that my husband and I could be called father and mother. We would be a real family with the same last name. It might not be a big deal to most of you who are reading this story, but to me it was way beyond joyous.

That day arrived when we went to the hospital and my water broke. I knew for sure that I would get to meet my baby in a few hours. They dressed me in a gown and hooked me up to all the proper machines. I could hear the baby's heart beat and I was getting so excited to see my baby even though the pain was getting unbearable. After eighteen and a half hours of pushing and enduring the pain, they took me into the delivery room and told me to push. Now the joy was becoming reality. It took only a few pushes and there he was. He was a nine pound six ounce baby boy. He cried and I knew that I would learn the sound of that cry and what it meant. I would learn when he was hurt, sad, hungry, and fussy. Lying there on the gurney listening to him cry, I waited patiently for my husband to bring him over for me to hold.

Wrapped in a blue, pink, and white stripped blanket, he nestled against my cheek and I gave him his first kiss. I was so tired, but the joy of seeing my baby for the first time took away the pain and the fatigue that gripped my body. Soon my husband was giving me each little detail of seeing him emerge from my body. He announced the weight and length and time our baby was born. He watched as they made his footprint and cleaned out his nose. I listened to a minute-by-minute report from my husband. Of course, we each saw a piece of ourselves reflected in his face. The excitement grew as we named him and he soon responded to his name.

I remember being tired and sleepy but the excitement was so joyous that neither my husband nor I could sleep while I was in the hospital. When we went home, the joy continued. Even though we had to get up several times in the middle of the night, when we saw that face we both knew it was worth it. We loved him and met all of his needs. Three years later, we had another son who again stole our heart and brought more joy into our life. We never thought that we could love him as much as the first baby, but we were so wrong. This baby was a blessing, beautiful and we love Him just as we did the first child. They are both grown now, but each time I see them walk into my house or hear their voices on the phone I have a joy that can't be expressed on paper. They are my heartbeat. They are the very soul of my being. They bring me joy.

When someone has wounded you, it can take away your zest for life. It is important to remember there are two kinds of joy: physical joy and spiritual joy. Physical joy does not last forever. It is like new toys on Christmas day. Soon that joy will disappear. Each one of us needs to know the spiritual joy that we can experience when we know we are loved and accepted even when we are wounded. When you have accepted Christ into your life, the Holy Spirit will give you the same kind of joyous experience. Joy is not just a smile or physical appearance; it is a peace in your heart. The only way to keep peace in your heart is to keep Christ on your mind. When all else fails, remember that He will take your problems and give you back your joy. The irony is, we do not totally believe God is going to take away the problem. Remember this one thing: "He is the God of Peace."

Philippians 4:4

"Always be full of Joy in the Lord."

Paul writes about joy in Philippians. Paul understood that God was in control. He knew that this is not the end of life but just the waiting place until God comes to get His people. Paul was in prison yet he had joy in his life and a connection with God that released him from the pain of being chained. He had faith and he totally concentrated on God's love that gave him joy. Paul knew that God was real and he did everything he could to make others believe in Him. He promised that God was coming back to take His people home. He reminded the people to not worry about anything, but pray about everything. Tell everyone what God has done for you. When you have been blessed and have experienced joy from God, remember to be joyous in your testimony to others.

To bring joy into your life, try this exercise. Make a list of all the things that worry you. Pray to God to take away your worries. Then leave them in God's hands.

The Joy of the Lord will bring a peace of mind that you will only experience when you truly trust the Lord.

Chapter 15

Forgiveness

A wounded spirit has to learn to forgive. I write this with a hesitant hand. This is one of the hardest things for me to practice. Over the last few years, my family has been through so much pain due to others who have wounded us financially and emotionally.

Without going through too much detail, I will share that my husband and I have lost money through investments that were planned to support us through our retirement. We also lost money from a business when someone stole from us. Keeping this in mind, how do you think you would feel about refiguring your future because funds are not available as expected? The whole process can be explained as stealing and deception. We worked our whole life and put away a nest egg to get us through the senior years. The money was our future. Why would someone do this to another person? Unfortunately, this person has done this to several other people. I will never understand how someone can steal and not feel guilty. Our only hope now is to get our money back through the legal system, which may or may not happen.

What do you do when you face the person who deceived you? Do you run up to them and throw your arms around them and say, "I forgive you for ruining my life?"

No, I can't do it right now. You can understand why I have had a huge problem with forgiveness.

I remember the first time I found out that someone had stolen from us. I called a friend of ours who was a minister. I told him about the person and asked if God was going to punish this person? He first laughed because he thought that I was not serious. Then I repeated my question. "It doesn't look like the legal system cares about the little business person. We are not getting the justice we deserve. I really want to know if God is going to punish this thief." Then he had me read these verses in the Bible:

Matthew 6: 24

"No one can serve two masters. For you will hate one and love the other, or be devoted to one and despise the other. You cannot serve both God and money."

Matthew 6: 20

"Unless you obey God you cannot enter into the kingdom of Heaven at all."

"Yes, this person will be punished," assured the minister. "God knows his heart and He will deal with him. You have to learn to forgive this person so you will not be judged, but will enter the Kingdom of Heaven."

The only word that came into my mind after this conversation was, "Thanks."

So we must forgive horrible people who have put us through months and years of pain and hardship? How can we forgive?

I remember the verse in Matthew that says we must love our enemies and pray for those who persecute us. If we do this, we will be acting as true children of our Father in Heaven. It applies to all of God's children: We must learn to forgive to get to Heaven.

Wow! This will take many prayers and daily readings of God's Word. There is no doubt that God tells me that I must forgive.

When we hold a grudge against the person that hurt us, we are not free. This person takes away a piece of our lives. You begin to think of ways to get even. You wish bad things would happen to that person and you spend precious time waiting for the right moment to say or do something to let them know how much they hurt you.

I do not wish to have this person take away any more of my happiness. I do not wish to have my life spent in court, recalling events that only make me furious. I do wish to have my money returned and to see justice done. Chances are this is not going to happen. I must learn to forgive with no expectations for the person or persons that have wounded us.

One of the most difficult stories I ever heard was one that impressed me so much that I had to order the video from the TV show host who was sharing the story. It is called *The Heart of Texas.*

Can you imagine forgiving a hit and run driver who just happened to hit YOUR six-year-old daughter? This is a true story that really happened in Texas. A car hit a little girl and the police could not find the driver who hit her. Months later, an old man drives up to the general store and there on the car is the paint from the car he hit. He was old, did not realize that he had hit anything and when the police took him into the station, he was not aware of the accident. The father of the young girl went to his house to talk to him. He noticed that the family lived in a little shack with little or no furniture. They were very poor and did not have enough food to eat. Their family was also poor and never expected to have more than God had given them.

This man shared the Lord with him and his family and listened to his story. The father prayed for him and then said, "I forgive you." He told the police that he did not want to press charges against this man. Wow! Could you do that? He explained that punishing this man would not bring back his daughter. He gathered his grown sons and grandchildren, called the pastor of the local church and told the story of the old man. The family needed clothes, food and jobs. The old man needed a place to live where he did not have to fight the elements of the weather. The needs of this family were great.

The father listed the problems and circumstances that surrounded the family and shared them with friends and family. Everyone was surprised that he would even talk to this man. "How could you possibly face this person?" asked family members. It was hard for his wife to understand, but he explained that God tells us we have to forgive. The end result gave the old man a place to live and food to eat.

This is going far beyond forgiveness. This is reading God's Word and living in the Word. What kind of Christian can step away from the situation that hurts deeply and turn it around to serve and witness for Christ? I would say most of us could not do what this man did. I am sure he had several hours of prayer in his special praying place to find God listening and urging him to do the right thing. He had to be convinced that his little girl was in Heaven and that he would one day see her again. He had to believe that God does what he says. When He said to love your enemies, He was serious.

I have learned that to forgive someone does not mean you must have a relationship with that person. We do not have to take the next step, as this father did. I personally think it is easier to forgive a person if you do not have to be around them. I think we visually remember facts and events when there is contact. If it means leaving a job, a church, a neighborhood or a family, do it. It will ease the pain.

Jesus came to give us inner strength and peace. When we continue to suffer because someone hurt us, we do not have the peace we need to make life a happy place for ourselves or our loved ones. The devil would love to see us suffer as we keep hate for others in our minds and heart. By forgiving and keeping your eyes on Christ, you will show Satan that he cannot control you. A friend recently reminded me of the following verse.

John 3:16-18

For God so loved the world that he gave his only Son, so that everyone who believes in him will not perish, but have eternal life. God did not send his Son into the world to condemn it, but to save it. There is no judgment awaiting those who trust him. But, those who do not trust him have already been judged for not believing in the only Son of God.

God forgives, but unless a person repents, God can not have a real relationship with them. They will not go to Heaven or have Eternal Life.

I chose Christ and I want him to remain in my life until the day He takes me out of this sinful world. I have prayed, and will allow myself to forgive the people who have hurt our family. I have to forgive and show forgiveness to criminals. I do not have to share a daily hour or minute with them. They are responsible for their own actions. God is in control.

I have also learned that I do not have to address people, such as the person who attacked me verbally in the hospital. This person has the anger problem and I do not have to address her lies unless she is willing to humble herself and come to me with an open heart and mind to hear the truth. I no longer feel the guilt of not being friends with those who hurt me. I choose positive experiences and positive people. I have forgiven her, however; I do feel sorry for her. She is full of anger and she still does not know the truth in the situation.

Loving personalities are important. We all need to have affirmation of worth. We need to inspire others to look inward for happiness. We need to smile, say hello and handle ourselves in a way that gives happiness to everyone we meet. Be considerate of others. Show others that you see, hear and understand that there are times when they hurt. It is okay to hurt. It is okay to show emotion. It is not okay to hurt others.

Stand strong. So, what have we learned from reading this information?

- ✓ We are all born for a reason. God made us for a reason.

- ✓ It really does not matter what people think of you. It is important what Christ thinks of you.

- ✓ The only person you need to please is God.

- ✓ It is important not to judge others because we do not know who they really are and how they have suffered.

- ✓ Take time to be good to everyone. You do not have to be their best friend, but take time to listen to those who need a listening ear.

- ✓ Know that we are all on a journey and our focus is to get to Heaven. Keep the faith and go forward allowing God to carry your load. Know that God loves you and can forgive anything that you have done against Him or someone else.

✓ Learn to love who you are. Do not let others negate your worth. Get out of abusive relationships. Learn to trust in God's love.

✓ There is joy in life. Do not let others take away your joy.

✓ There is hope of eternal life. There is hope for a better way of living. You just have to look for it.

✓ You must learn to forgive those who have hurt you.

Look at your life. Are you getting what you give in life? Are you surrounding yourself with people who have strength? Are you taking time to fill your cup? Do you take time to rest and fill your soul with positive thoughts and activities that make you strong? Are you willing to seek professional help to get rid of an addiction? These are important questions that will help the wounded spirit to heal.

What most of us have never known is that there is Spiritual warfare going on in this worldly kingdom. It is a war between Satan and God. Satan will try to make you believe that God does not exist. He will twist your mind and make you dance to his music. Satan is always attacking. We must stand strong and not believe his lies. He uses people to drive Christians away from their belief. He makes things look so inviting that people will not believe God.

This world is a battlefield of the minds. We believe what we see on TV and what we read in the paper. We adjust our thoughts to make it right for what **we** want. People are not reading God's Word and are not listening to what God wants for us. He does not want us to suffer or have this spiritual warfare. He wants everyone to go to Heaven, but Satan wills us pain and promises us a good life that involves sin. Satan gives us the baggage that holds us to this world.

Satan tells us that we are not the physical sex that we were born with. Somehow, we think it is okay to change sexes because God got it wrong. Were we born to kill, steal, cheat, abuse, lie and hurt others by keeping secrets? The answer is YES!

We are all born sinners. One sin is as bad as another. Remember, God did not tell you to do these things. We do these things because we have a sinful nature. Thus, the warfare begins.

God gives us a brain to choose what is right and what is wrong. Whom will I choose to follow and believe today? If I repeatedly choose to cross the street in the middle of a busy highway, chances are I will soon be hit. It is my choice. I know better but I continue to make a bad choice. If I choose to continue to lie to my family and friends, soon I will think it is okay to lie about everything. It is not a sin anymore. If I choose to cheat on my spouse and do not get caught once or twice, then maybe it is okay to do this. If I steal from a store, and no one ever catches me, then it is okay because I pay taxes and I deserve to take this from this store. Everyone can make excuses for sin. People CHOOSE to sin. People CHOOSE to listen to Satan.

If you have suffered from life experiences, then you know what it is like to be in a spiritual war. If someone hurt you, wounded you, gave you grief and sorrow, it was not God, it was Satan. He can tear at your mind and say things that are evil. Satan will bring pain that causes pride, sin, and disbelief. He will change you from a believer to a non-believer who adjusts the rules and laws to fit your needs. You have free will, but you will believe what Satan tells you. It will be all about you and Satan will allow you to believe that you have the right to please yourself and no one else. If you believe in the sin, then you do not care if you hurt the ones who love you and pray for you.

A person chooses to take drugs; they are not born this way. They have a choice to say no. People choose to be child molesters even though they know it is wrong. They are not born this way. People choose to be prostitutes; they are not born this way. People are not born to continue to sin once they learn what is right and wrong. Once a person knows God and sees His Word, then God holds that person accountable and he or she must be obedient to God's law. Too often, they choose to continue to sin and obey Satan. Please note that Satan's laws are lies and will destroy any chances of spending eternity in Heaven.

God will not allow Satan's followers to enter the kingdom of Heaven. Sinful people who continue to sin, will say that there is no God. This is the destructive power of sin. Remember, every moral decision determines who controls your life.

You can heal your spirit by choosing to follow God's original plan for humans living here on this earth. You can choose to follow God's plan for your life. Pray, trust and obey. Ask God for His will to be done in your life. Start reading the New Testament where Jesus comes to earth to take away our sins and find someone to help you study His Word. Think positively about yourself and remember that God's love is there for you even when you move away from Him. He will take away the worry and the fear that surrounds you. Pray to God when Satan tempts you to turn away from the reality of God's love. Pray expecting that God will hear your prayers. Know that He is real and He can save you from your sin.

Take time for yourself. You're not on this journey alone. Someone is walking beside you. Learn to love all God has made and find the happiness He has designed for you. God has a plan and His plan is that you are worth saving and spending eternity in Heaven and not Hell.

YOU HAVE A CHOICE!

God bless everyone who has read this book and chooses to allow God to be in control of his or her spiritual life.

I hope I will share eternity with all of you.

Visit

LSKingBooks.com

Or

Email the author at:

Linda@LSKingBooks.com

Other Publications by LS King

No Ordinary Woman (ISBN: 978-0-9824373-0-8) – The true story of a woman who survived the great depression, WW II, divorce, and two marriages, all while building a successful business. The love of her life was an alcoholic and she had to work hard to support her two young children. She was a warm, wonderful woman who sometimes gave away more money than she made. She shared her success story with women everywhere and encouraged them to be strong both spiritually and physically. She was generous to everyone she met; was a mother to many children. She was my mother and I share her diary with you and you will see that she was certainly ***No Ordinary Woman***.

Lady Bray (ISBN: 978-0-9824373-8-4) – In a lifetime you will meet many people. Some you will remember and some you will forget. Lady Bray is a true story about Rosalie Bray, and one that you will remember. Born in the early 1900's in Indiana, Rosalie's life spanned ninety-nine years of family tragedies and triumphs. The book starts in her early years and brings history alive through the eyes of a spirited young woman as she makes her way through life.

Divine Interventions (Coming soon) – Mrs. King felt it very important to share with her readers all the miracles she and her friends have experienced. You may or may not believe in angels, but after you read this book you will understand that God is in control. Each story is true and guaranteed to pique your interest. If you enjoy reading the mysteries of how God works, you will not want to miss reading ***Divine Interventions.***